Praise for Client Centric

"This powerful, practical book teaches you the inner game of success, how to unlock your true sales potential, and how to make more sales, faster and easier than ever before."
Brian Tracy, author of *Advanced Selling Skills*

"A mind-expanding book explaining the secrets of hypnotic influence. Easy reading, easy to implement, and easy to get more sales with it."
Dr. Joe Vitale, author of *Hypnotic Writing*

"I encourage anyone wishing to apply millionaire thinking to their business to read Client Centric. It provides a unique approach to marketing and wealth building."
T. Harv Eker, author of *Secrets of the Millionaire Mind*

"Anyone doing business in our new economy will benefit from these lessons. Simple ways to leverage your customer's experience to generate a lot more business."
Joel Comm, author of *Twitter Power*

CLIENT CENTRIC

CLIENT CENTRIC

Grow Your Business With An Amazing Customer Experience

Randy Charach

PARAGON
PUBLISHING

ISBN-13: 978-1-988776-00-2
ISBN-10: 1988776007

Disclaimer: The information included in this book is the opinion of the author. It is for educational purposes only and not meant as a substitute for the advice of a lawyer, accountant or any licensed professional. This book contains advice that, regardless of the author's results and experience, may not produce the same results, or any results, for you. The author makes no guarantee, expressed or implied, that by following the advice, the readers will get the same results, as there are several factors and variables that come into play regarding any given situation. By reading this book, you assume all risks associated with using the advice, data, and suggestions and the author and publisher cannot be held responsible for anything that may occur as a result of putting this information into action in any way.

This book is dedicated to my

Mom, Dad, Wife and Kids.

You were, are, and always will be
the inspiration for all I do.

CONTENTS

ACKNOWLEDGMENTS

Deepest gratitude to the sales-person, service professional and entrepreneur who realize...

...sales, marketing and branding are crucial elements of the customer experience.

...providing a consistent and thoughtful customer experience is the most important aspect of any business.

I would also like to express my gratitude to the crafty salespeople, impatient customer service reps, uninformed financial pros, negligent medical professionals, careless restaurant staff, and all the others out there who provide sub-par experiences for us regular people...

...thank you for teaching me to lower my expectations.

...thank you for showing me how important it is to take responsibility and conduct my own due diligence.

...thank you for inspiring me to write this book, and being a catalyst in my pursuit of excellence.

And most importantly...
I would like to thank my wife Chana and my four daughters Leilani, Shira, Kyla, and Talia. They patiently allowed me to

take time away from them to pursue my passion in writing this book.

Thank you to my editor Philip Espinosa, for your patience, skill, and thoughtful guidance throughout this entire process. And to my proofreader Susan Soares for her fine work.

Thank you to my insightful and generous beta readers, Jeff Bliss, Chana Charach, Alain Guez, and Jim Rogers.

Thank you to Vern Jurovich, Elliot Laskin, Gary Lenett, John Lutrin, Judy Miller, Neil Pollock, Anthony Smith, and Stephan Stavrakis, who provided valuable opinions on the content and title of this book.

Your insights and thoughts helped make this work of passion the best it can be.

And, thank you to my readers who will now deliver an amazing customer experience to grow their business.

INTRODUCTION

What This Book Is About

Let's break it down, shall we?

This book is based on the experience of a twelve-year-old kid (that was me), who began earning money as a magician and became a self-made millionaire by the age of twenty-four.

I realized early on "all business is show business." The client experience I provide begins long before I step on stage.

As a successful entrepreneur many years later, I'm sharing these hard-won insights with you. Now, you too can grow your business by being client centric.

In a sentence, this book is about attracting better clients and bigger sales by focusing on your customer's experience.

To be client centric, you focus your business activities on your customer. This focus begins with their first exposure to your brand and remains present and consistent throughout the lifetime of the relationship.

This book will show you how to deliver an amazing and hypnotic customer experience to grow your business.

A hypnotic experience is a state of consciousness associated with focused attention and the willingness to respond to suggestion.

The methods shared in this book are based on sound, psychological principles I developed over decades as a professional magician, mentalist, hypnotist, and entrepreneur.

In simple terms, you'll discover how to apply mindset, messaging, and marketing to help your business thrive.

Who Should Read This Book

This book is written for the salesperson, the entrepreneur, and the professional.

Generally, people prefer to do business with a brand that provides an experience superior to their competitors.

You should know, regardless of your business or profession, you're in sales.

Read this book if you're:

- Passionate about growing your business.

- Ready to position your brand to focus on your highest value prospects and clients.

- Ready to become the only choice when your ideal client compares you to the competition.

Read this book if you want to attract and retain high-value clients in this digital age.

Why I Wrote This Book

From age eighteen to twenty, my life was a mess.

Most of my days and nights were spent in severe physical agony. The pain woke me up early in the morning. The pain medication kept me drowsy all day.

My family doctor's only explanation was that it was all in my mind. He came to this conclusion after sending me for an x-ray. I knew this wasn't the case.

It came to a point where I wanted to die as a way to end the suffering. Instead, I asked a lot of questions of a lot of people. Through research and tenacity, I discovered a more detailed type of x-ray, called a CT scan.

You can't imagine how delighted I was after the scan to learn I had a bone tumor. Yippee, I have a tumor. Really, I was prepared to lose my leg to relieve the pain. Once the doctor at the hospital explained it was a benign tumor and could be removed, I was even more delighted. It wasn't cancerous, and the end of my suffering was now in plain sight. Or, was it?

The surgeon removed the tumor and told me the pain it caused was over. What followed was like waking up out of a nightmare and going straight into two years of hell. In the first operation, the surgeon failed to remove the entire tumor. It grew back a few months later.

My dear father flew with me to Mayo Clinic. They were supposed to be the best. They cut out a lot of my leg and hip bone but didn't remove the tumor. Apparently, they failed to re-scan the area prior to surgery. The tumor had shifted.

A year later, after recovering from the second surgery, I had a third operation. The tumor was finally successfully removed. Nightmare over. Let the scarring begin!

It took me many years to realize how emotionally scarred I was. Now, three decades later, writing this book is a realization of how these mishaps affected my life. For better and for worse.

For many years, I was intolerant of mistakes, made by myself and others. I still have this trait, yet have learned to harness it in a healthier way. Still today, I suffer from perfectionism. And, I'm still intolerant of people who don't demonstrate reasonable care.

Are you picking up what I'm putting down here?

My mindset had turned to extreme negativity towards whatever I perceived as incompetence. I was unforgiving of myself and others.

This isn't a self-help book. It's a book to help you grow your business. I wrote it, based on my obsession with excellence. This obsession stemmed from my distaste for negligent treatment by people who were considered professionals in their field.

I wrote this book because I realize the tumor experience led to my emotional and financial wealth. The money came first. It has taken a lot longer to realize the root of the negative thinking and reprogram my mind to be more tolerant and forgiving.

My businesses and career have created wealth due to an approach based on a burning desire to amaze my customers. To leave no stone unturned when seeking a solution. To not let my clients down, as several doctors let me down many years ago.

This book combines my passion for providing an amazing customer experience with a lifetime of experience in marketing and show business.

I wrote this book because all business is show business.

I wrote this book because all experience exists in the mind.

I wrote this book because we're all selling something to someone.

I wrote this book to share with you, not how to sell your product or service. Rather, how to sell the experience of doing business with your brand.

How to Use This Book

This book is organized in three parts. Each part sets the stage for the foundation of a successful business. Each part builds upon the previous. These parts are mindset, message, and marketing.

When these parts are combined as instructed in this book, your brand will deliver an amazing customer experience. In return, you'll attract better clients and make bigger sales.

Start with part one and go through this book in the order in which it's presented. This is an evergreen book. Meaning, the principles will never change. At least, not in my lifetime.

For the most part, I've avoided naming specific entities as they are subject to change. When a company or website is mentioned, it will likely still be around whenever you read this book.

Your customer experience is determined by your mindset, and the experience in the mind of your client. Your brand attracts customers to you with its message. Your marketing shares your message in a way which will influence and persuade others to do business with you.

Use this book to set a foundation for your brand. Apply the methods contained within to make your competition disappear. It's not magic, but it works like magic. Now, start reading, so you can grow your business by providing an amazing customer experience.

PART ONE: MINDSET

"Everything is mindset, and mindset is everything."

CHAPTER ONE: YOUR MINDSET

When most people try to grow their businesses, they gravitate towards the latest marketing tactics or sales techniques. They get excited about the latest software to automate their business, hoping to free up more time.

All these ways of growing, expanding, and providing more freedom in our lives are great. However, these are external methods, and while essential to our growth, they need to be secondary to our way of thinking about reaching higher levels of success.

Internal factors are comprised of your beliefs about the world and your attitudes about people and the manner in which they operate. These factors, along with your opinions and habits of thinking, have the greatest impact on your business success and personal well-being.

We'll go into detail on the external factors related to sales and marketing and systemizing your business. Before that, it's essential we examine the foundation of your mindset.

Internal factors, like mindset, help to determine the success of your business. Factors like intelligence and ability, while important, don't guarantee success. Rather, our mindset, our belief about our abilities, plays the most fundamental role in fueling our success.

What is Mindset?

Your mindset is your collection of beliefs. It includes ideas about primary qualities like your intelligence, abilities, and personality.

Many people are smart and gifted, yet they still don't reach their potential. I wonder what held them back. If it's not their intelligence or talent, then what is it? More than likely, it's their mindset.

We all have beliefs about ourselves. We have a certain view regarding our knowledge. You may believe you're not smart because you didn't perform well in school. Some people think our grades in school determine how smart we are. Not true.

This thinking shows up in our lives in thoughts like, "I'm not smart because I didn't get good grades. Only smart people succeed. I'm not intelligent, therefore, I can never be at the top of my game."

This mindset is negative thinking. It ignores the fact that intelligence is much more than just how well you did in school. Many of our world business leaders and top thinkers did poorly in school or even dropped out of school. I barely scraped through school myself.

Maybe you did great in school, but you have a negative mindset about certain talents and abilities. This mindset has been holding you back from reaching your highest potential. It's stopping you from achieving the success you desire and deserve.

For example, like others, you might fear public speaking. This fear may go back to a speech you had to make as a child or teenager, or when you presented your thesis in college. Perhaps you had stage fright and froze in front of the audience. Since that day, you've told yourself, "I'm a terrible public speaker."

Just think how that has held you back from connecting with others in your current business situation. Think of the new contacts you could make and the number of people you could persuade if you broke through that one self-limiting belief.

Your negative, self-limiting beliefs are in your subconscious mind, and they hold you back. We all have them. We just looked at two examples of common damaging mindsets. Those were around our beliefs about our intelligence and abilities.

These are examples of negative mindsets that hold us back. The good news is we can shift our mindset. We have the potential to change our mindset and reach new levels of success we never before imagined possible.

You may not be aware of your mindset and beliefs. It's not always easy to identify them. I'm talking about that inner voice, the thoughts that flow through your mind all day long.

Meet Your Mental DJ

Those negative thoughts come from a voice in our head, often referred to in psychology as the inner-critic, or in spiritual circles, the monkey-mind. These thoughts are a nagging manifestation of negativity that plays in your mind on a continuous repeat mode behind your conscious thoughts.

It's a voice telling you that you're wrong, you're not good enough, and you'll fail. It acts as your judge and jury condemning you at every turn.

I call this your mental DJ. It's like being at a party. You can accept the song choices of the DJ, make requests of your own, or even bring your own music.

Now, some people are aware of this mental DJ while others aren't. Being conscious of this mental DJ doesn't mean you're equipped to deal with it. Many people who are aware, make the mistake of thinking it's their true-self doing this negative talking. They identify with this voice, and this holds them back.

Since we all have this mental DJ, we need to find a way to use it to our advantage. The first step in transforming the negative self-talk into positive self-talk is to understand we absolutely can do something about it. We can take steps to own this mental DJ.

The good news about our mindset is we can develop it, train it, and evolve it, so that it helps us.

Instead of your unconscious or subconscious mind where your mental DJ exists, you'll now have a super-conscious mind to help push you to the next level of success. Your super-conscious mind can control and override these seemingly random thoughts going through your mind on a continuous loop all day.

Even the smallest shift in awareness and habits of thinking will make profound differences in your life. You'll take control of your mindset and achieve more than you ever thought possible.

Let's start with an awareness of those thoughts holding us back. We'll then change the way we think about this in a process called reframing. This reframing is the action you take to support your new awareness and a new way of thinking.

This exercise will be fun for you. This habit of reframing is something everyone needs to do. Regardless of how evolved you already are, or how well you believe you have all this mindset stuff covered, you'll benefit from going through these exercises. I urge you to do them.

Are you ready? We'll do this right now. I'll guide you in clearing your mind to help you become more aware of your thoughts. So, get comfortable. Turn off all distractions. Take a deep breath in through your nose and out through your mouth.

Don't worry. Although I'm an accomplished hypnotist, I'm not about to hypnotize you. I promise not to put you into a trance and have you wake up feeling compelled to buy more of my books. That would be evil.

Okay, whenever you're about to do an exercise involving thought, take a moment to slowly breathe in through your nose, and out through your mouth, and notice the calmness it brings.

Your mindset, your way of looking at things forms your foundation for everything else. Just as an optometrist can help you see more clearly, this exercise and new habit will help you think more clearly.

It's time for you to flex your imagination and go through a mental exercise. Ask yourself the following questions.

Does your ideal life include more vacations, more money, or better relationships?

When considering each item, take another deep breath in through your nose, out through your mouth, and close your eyes while thinking about what it all means to you.

Does financial freedom mean having your house paid off within the next five years? Does it mean having enough money to send your kids to the best private school or a top university? Does it mean moving from a five-figure to a six-figure, or a six-figure to seven-figure, income?

As you're thinking about each of these, pay close attention to those thoughts in your mind. Are those ideas helping or hurting you right now? Are they your friend or your enemy?

Is your mental DJ pushing its way through to your conscious mind, or are these thoughts progressive and helpful ideas? Are you hearing, "I'll pick up five new high-value clients next month." Or, are you hearing, "Who the hell are you kidding, that will never happen?"

Many people have trouble differentiating between the mental DJ and their actual thoughts. This may be the case for you if you haven't begun to deal with your negative thinking.

The point of this exercise is for you to notice your inner voice, your mental DJ.

Static and Dynamic Mindsets

A static mindset means you believe your character, intelligence, and other abilities are fixed. They cannot change. They are unchanging parts of who you are, ingrained within you.

You've probably heard the saying, "People can't change." Statements such as this support the belief we have a static mindset. One of the key characteristics of someone with a static mindset is a constant need to prove themselves.

They feel since they only have a set amount of intelligence, personality, or talent, it's important to put on display all they have. These people are often consumed with proving they have worth to others.

People who have an unhealthy concern with static labels, identify themselves in relation to their intelligence and their abilities. They may even let notions of how fun they are influence their identity.

A dynamic mindset is one where an individual sees characteristics, knowledge, and skills, as always developing and evolving. Unlike the static mindset, a dynamic mindset doesn't compel you to impress others. You're confident in your current abilities. You know you can change and grow with experience and practice.

Your qualities are clearly not static. It doesn't matter if others believe you lack certain qualities. First of all, it's merely their perception. Even if there's truth to this perception, it doesn't matter. We know we can always grow and learn.

One key to succeeding in any field is the absolute willingness and desire to understand new concepts and welcome change. This tendency is why a dynamic mindset is associated with success.

A static mindset is dominant in a person who becomes excellent at something and then stays stagnant and fails to make further progress. The person will either succeed with a task at first try or give up in disappointment. Their mental DJ has already informed them about what they are or aren't good at doing.

A dynamic mindset is dominant in people who accept new challenges and solve problems along the way. We can see how these mindsets reveal themselves to us in our own and other people's lives.

Think about the people we knew who had everything going for them. They were intelligent, talented, and had charming personalities. Later in life, as you stalk them on social media, you discover their life didn't turn out the way you would've expected.

It's as if they took off early and then fizzled out right away or just remained stagnant. In most cases, those people had a static mindset and just couldn't continue growing and evolving.

In other instances, when you reconnect with someone with a dynamic mindset, they have likely achieved more than you would ever have thought possible.

Perhaps there are people like this around you now in your work environment. You see people who are thriving, yet they appear void of even the most basic skills, have a quirky personality, or lack talent.

These are people with dynamic mindsets. They have a tenacity about them and believe they can grow and expand in any area of their life.

I want you to invest, as I have, quality time to understand the difference between static and dynamic mindsets. Identify where you have either a dynamic and open or a static and closed mindset.

As we continue through this chapter, we'll work on any area where you're stuck.

Our goal is to get you into the process of a new and improved way of thinking.

3 Steps to Dynamic Thinking

So far, I've been referring to static and dynamic mindsets regarding personality characteristics.

It's important to recognize mindsets aren't fixed, they are situational. One mindset may come into play in certain situations, and another at different times in your life.

An example is when you're facing a new situation where you're unsure of yourself and not confident. Here, you're more likely to adopt a static mindset. You're likely to have more of a dynamic mindset in activities where you're confident or experienced.

Defaulting to a static mindset, whether situationally or for a significant portion of your life, will limit your success, health, and happiness in the long term.

With your new understanding of the difference between a dynamic and static mindset, let's take steps to move you toward a more dynamic mindset.

Step 1: Identify Your DJ. Earlier, I spoke of the voice of your mental DJ. You were likely aware of its existence and just never gave it much thought. The first step toward greater understanding of your mindset is for you to identify that voice and notice when you hear it. It's when that mental DJ shows up, you're in that mental state of a static mindset.

It's simple to practice awareness. Start by just noticing the voice when you hear it. Then identify what happened just before those negative thoughts. It's like making a diagnosis of a headache. To discover its origin, you may need to think back to what you were doing, or who you were with, just before.

If you're having trouble identifying your mental DJ, think back for clues. Think about the times you've doubted yourself and heard voices in your head saying things like, "I can't do this." Going forward, pay attention to when you're focusing on failure and not focusing on success.

The static mindset will show up in situations when you're trying something new or challenging. For example, now as you learn to be more client centric, don't allow this mindset to hold you back.

As you evolve into this new way of selling, you'll come across new ideas and challenges. Decide in advance you're able to do it. Be cautious of the mental DJ and push it away when it shows up, tempting you to believe you cannot do something.

Now things can get exciting. Once you recognize this voice, you can learn to control it. The way you interpret challenges, obstacles, or criticism is up to you.

Step 2: Reframe Your Thoughts. Recognizing the source of the voice in one's head is the most challenging step for most people. Now, you need to control that voice after all these years of accepting its current form. So, here's a shortcut, a magic trick you can use to reframe your thoughts.

By the way, in case you're not aware, I started performing magic shows as a young child. Performing magic tricks is now second nature to me. It's something I've done thousands of times. Granted, the following isn't a typical magic trick. Nevertheless, of all the magic tricks I could teach you, this one is the most powerful.

Imagine a time when you gave advice to a friend. You wouldn't use a harsh and critical voice when trying to help someone out. So, why is your mental DJ so hard on you when you're dealing with your thoughts and issues? It need not, and should not be.

Here's the mental magic trick. When you recognize your mental DJ isn't playing the song you want, imagine you're giving advice to a friend. We're so much harder on ourselves than we are on other people. So, again, here's the trick: Instead of talking to yourself in a nasty manner, take control of the mental DJ and imagine you're giving advice to a good friend.

Pretend that voice is your partner or a family member talking to you about themselves. Then imagine you giving them advice and rephrase those negative statements in your mind to yourself.

Here's an example. If you find yourself thinking you can't make a sale because you lack the experience, reframe the message in your mind. Frame it as if a friend were telling you they cannot make a sale because they lack the experience.

What would you say to your friend?

You might say, "Hey! Your experience isn't the most important factor here, and you got this!" You give them a positive, motivating dose of encouragement.

Do the same for yourself. Change the initial thought of "I can't make this sale because I'm not experienced enough" to "I got this." Remember, you aren't static. You're always learning, you're dynamic, so, of course you got this.

Makes sense, doesn't it? Learn to recognize static statements and practice turning them into dynamic statements. Make this a conscious effort. Do it, and it will become a habit ingrained in your subconscious.

Step 3: Take New Action. The third and final, most crucial step, is to take action on what you just reframed.

Start by asking yourself, "What challenges can I accept to nurture my dynamic mindset? What challenges have I been avoiding and what opportunities have I been missing?"

Examine one of the roadblocks in your life and take another shot at it. This time, turn your fixed mindset around. Choose something work related, or in your personal life. Choose something you've shied away from or where you feel you've failed. Do this and experience turning something around in your life.

For example, maybe you spend so much energy focused on acquiring new clients that your health has suffered. You don't allow yourself time to exercise. You rush through meals and eat unhealthy food because it's fast and convenient. How can you challenge yourself to make time in your life to be healthier?

Perhaps that's not your issue at all. Maybe, what's holding you back is spending so much time each day at the gym or cooking food, there's no time left for you to work on your business. Your priorities are out of whack! Maybe there's an important client you've been meaning to contact and just haven't found the time because you're allowing yourself to procrastinate. Every time you're about to move forward in your business, you find a distraction that seems more important at the moment.

Until now, you may not have even noticed a roadblock existed. Pinpoint one issue and start there. Make it a challenge. Turn it around. Switch your mindset from static to dynamic on one issue at a time and watch how your business grows, and your life improves.

You'll notice you use a static mindset in some circumstances and a dynamic mindset in others. For example, you might have a dynamic mindset for a goal to grow your business, yet for having a healthier lifestyle, you might have more of a static mindset. Take some time as you work on your mindset to identify where your static mindset holds you back.

You can change this when you practice reframing. You'll take those same negative thoughts and frame them as dynamic mindset statements.

Remember the magic trick: Imagine yourself giving a good friend advice. That mental image will help you reframe your thoughts.

From the reframe statements, is there one area of your life you can work on right now? If you want to be healthier, is there a challenge you could take on to help move your life in a healthier direction?

Perhaps you've always wanted to try swimming. I only learned how to swim in my forties, and it was difficult for me to get from one end of the pool to the other. Realizing swimming is an excellent form of exercise, I took lessons and learned how to swim. Now I swim for an hour, non-stop, three times a week. This new skill came from reframing what my mental DJ told me. I changed the thinking from it was too late, to "Hell, no, I can, and I will learn to swim." And I did.

In fact, just yesterday, I overheard a man at the club where I swim, talking about how swimming is like learning a language. You need to learn it when you're young. Sure, this skill may be easier to learn when you're younger, but don't let that stop you. I moved past this fixed, limiting, negative, static mindset. You can too.

So, forget about all these preconceived notions.

If your goal is to increase your income by two hundred percent, what is one thing you can take on that your static mindset has held you back from doing?

Write down one challenge you can work on today. By the way, in this book, you'll discover many ways you can increase your income. My client centric methods work. They've been successful for me and many others I've coached, time and time again.

When you stop thinking about selling products and services, and shift to selling the experience embraced by you and your brand, your income will increase. Much more than you can even imagine. You'll also find it will be more fun for you and your clients as your business expands. This will lead you to better clients and bigger sales.

The Source of Negative Thinking

Most people start off working for someone else. I was fortunate I became an entertainer at a young age. I worked for myself from the beginning, and my mindset has always been that of an entrepreneur.

Working for someone else is fundamentally different from working for yourself. An employee mindset and an entrepreneur mindset are two different animals.

If you've been working for many years for someone else, you may not even realize there's a difference in mindset. Also, the longer you've worked as an employee, the harder it is to change your mindset and think like an entrepreneur. It's crucial you do, though, since the employee mindset won't serve you well. In fact, it will work against you.

Before we dive into the source of your mindset, let's take a look at the fundamental differences between the employee and the entrepreneur mindset.

As an employee, you might blame others and share responsibility. Regarding the vision of the company, you typically focus on short-term, task-oriented activities. Making decisions isn't your sole responsibility. Your training and continued mandate to learn are specific to your role in the company. You're required to follow the rules, not set them.

As an entrepreneur, all roads lead back to you. You learn to create something from nothing. You focus on both short and long-term outcomes. Without all the answers, you still need to make decisions and face uncertainty. You wear many hats and continuously learn and grow.

Many people who own their own business still operate with an employee mindset.

So, whether you're a financial advisor, chiropractor, optometrist, entertainer, speaker, tractor salesperson, or dog trainer, if you want to grow and become client centric, you need to think like an entrepreneur.

Let's take this to another level. Let's look at the difference in mindset between the small business owner or independent sales or service professional, and the entrepreneur.

Small business owners think in micro terms.

They know their business and who their ideal client is and strive to make their clients happy. They are more comfortable with predictability and tend to be more calculated and conservative in their decisions. They focus more on short-term goals and outcomes. They manage their employees, work with their clients, and attend networking events.

Their goal is to keep the status quo or grow just enough so they don't go backward in their business.

The entrepreneur is always looking for the next big idea. They live in a dynamic mindset, knowing anything is possible. They take action, embrace risk, and move forward without knowing the outcome. They are more long-term oriented, philosophical about business, and focus on growth and profitability. They work more ON their business than IN their business and surround themselves with experts from whom they can learn.

I think you'll agree, cultivating an entrepreneur mindset is right for you, so I'll help you do that right now.

You likely already have as your basic foundation an entrepreneur mindset, or you wouldn't have invested in this book. You, like me, are also likely to be of the mind you can always improve and grow even when you have the right foundation in place.

Your limiting beliefs come from your life experience. To fit into society as an adult, you've been conditioned to think in static mindset terms, especially with thoughts as they relate to intelligence, money, and authority.

The first step is for you to recognize your beliefs and attitudes that limit you. To do this, you need to look at where your mindset originated.

Knowing how someone else ticks is a huge advantage in sales and marketing. Understanding how we tick is the first step in understanding others.

Even if you believe you're of one hundred percent entrepreneur mindset, still do these exercises. My methods of gaining insight will serve you well going forward.

When we took part in an aptitude or IQ test as kids, many of us would then identify ourselves with the results.

Many adults have developed an identity based on this perceived level of intelligence, and have gone through life with a static mindset based on these early and often irrelevant results.

Whatever our early education led us to believe, whether it's "I'm gifted, and the teacher likes me" or "I'm an idiot, and I'll never be smart," we turn these beliefs over to that mental DJ which we switch on when faced with challenges.

Now, we can unlearn this habit of thinking. We can cultivate a dynamic mindset which is a more evolved way of thinking.

Another critical area of life where limiting beliefs hurt us is money and finances. These ideas often originate within the family based on what parents say to their children.

Typical limiting beliefs include thoughts like:

- Money is the root of all evil.

- People with money cheated to get it.

- There's never enough money.

- You have to sacrifice if you want to buy something expensive.

- We'll never retire.

These limiting beliefs often will express feelings of guilt, hopelessness, or scarcity around money. Early educational experiences also play a part in shaping limiting beliefs about what work is.

The current education system in most countries focuses on learning whatever is needed to pass an exam. There's little emphasis on training young people to become successful adult entrepreneurs, freelance workers, sales and service professionals, or small business owners.

This old model involves working for a set period of time doing tasks assigned to you by a boss. For this job, you receive pay of an agreed-upon amount. Frequently, an hourly rate. Through obeying your boss, working hard, and producing value for the company, you might receive a better position or a pay increase.

This model fundamentally clashes with the entrepreneur mindset. Rewards are reserved for workers who obey. Success in this model is tied to an ability to produce for others and to minimize risk. Accepting risks and taking on challenges are fundamental to success as an entrepreneur.

Here are some other ideas you may also have internalized from your education.

Our conditioning to obey authority is learned early on in our lives. In fact, this inclination to follow others dates way back into early civilization. It's ingrained in us. It's wired into our DNA.

Those who lead are successful in life. They question authority and don't let self-limiting behavior impede success.

Hey, I'm not trying to invoke a revolution here. I don't want you to start protesting or running red lights and telling the police officer you just don't care. I think you get where I'm going with this. Relate it to the context of learning to be client centric from a dynamic mindset.

As kids in school, we were given instructions, provided examples, and shown demonstrations. We read and learned about concepts before applying them. We began with theory and then evolved into actually doing something.

In many ways, this is the opposite of the entrepreneur mindset in which we often try out something new as the first step and then put the pieces of the puzzle together after getting our feet wet.

As we grew up and went through school, our grades and performance were compared to others. That early exposure to comparisons can be toxic. It encourages us to compare ourselves to others as a way of determining success.

If you still find yourself with thoughts such as, "I'm a better salesperson than Jerry, but not as good as Anne," then it's time to say goodbye to that way of thinking. It's just going to hold you back.

Stop comparing and judging.

This is what I love about hypnosis. In a hypnotic state, we bypass that critical faculty and create selective thinking. We tap into our subconscious mind which doesn't judge, compare, or criticize.

We also develop a non-critical mind through meditation and practice of religions such as Buddhism. There are many paths to expanding your mind and priming it for success.

How to Expand Your Mind

Previously, you identified and reframed old mindsets that no longer serve your best interests. You learned key insights about yourself related to the employee mindset. You compared small business ownership thinking to entrepreneurship. With this insight, you're now ready to look deeper into the entrepreneur mindset and adopt the characteristics that will make the biggest impact on your success.

We'll now look at some of the characteristics and habits of entrepreneurs.

As we do this, think about people you know who exhibit these habits and whether you display them yourself.

When something goes sideways, an entrepreneur will reframe things in a new way by repositioning or rephrasing.

Instead of thinking, "How can I avoid this problem?" they'll ask themselves "How can I correct this issue?"

You can't always achieve success on your first try. One of the entrepreneur mindset key habits is that of trying and trying again. Through ups and downs and bends and turns, tenacity will always prevail.

Entrepreneurs expect surprises and setbacks no matter how much they plan. They learn from these so-called failures and move forward. This manner of thinking is that of a dynamic mindset.

A person with a static mindset is likely to give up when they encounter a setback. Because of their perceived limitations, the static mindset person will see a challenge as a personal failing.

An entrepreneur mindset allows you to uncover the lessons hidden in each setback to grow stronger and move on. Just like the dynamic mindset, an essential characteristic of the entrepreneur mindset is perseverance and tenacity. I love that word, tenacity, and first learned its true meaning in acting school. And then, to a greater extent, during my first one hundred auditions where I didn't receive the part!

Entrepreneurs tackle challenges head-on and don't beat themselves up over failures. They don't give up just because something is difficult.

People with an entrepreneur mindset don't do everything themselves. They reach out and seek help from others who can do things for them. They are good at spotting talent.

It's important for you to recognize your skills and abilities. Sometimes, even though you can do something or improve on something, it's simply best to have someone else do it for you.

Constantly ask yourself, "Is this the best use of my time right now?"

There's no need to focus on things and spend time on activities which aren't necessarily a priority or the best use of your time. Instead of doing low-level work, focus on planning your business, and building relationships.

Develop your love of learning. There's something to learn from everyone. Have a hunger for knowledge and new ways of thinking and doing things. Embrace new technology, new ideas, new concepts, and theories. Welcome change.

Are you open-minded when it comes to learning? Do you find it fun tackling new technology, and do you embrace change? If not, I challenge you to adopt this mindset of always learning and growing. Again, I feel you wouldn't be here if this weren't already your attitude. I want to reinforce how important it is for you to continue with this mindset. As you grow, you won't only be comfortable with change, you'll be a leader when it comes to making change for yourself and others around you.

Rely on your gut instinct when making decisions. I happen to be highly intuitive and continue to develop my intuition. I'll also be the first to admit, yet perhaps not recognize, I'm not always right. At the end of the day, I'll go with what I feel over what I think.

It's best to combine non-emotional, analytical calculations with your instincts when making decisions. An eclectic approach to decision making is a dynamic-oriented mindset working in combination with an entrepreneur mindset. This, along with trusting your instincts. Besides that, there's the willingness to accept a calculated risk and take action.

As true entrepreneurs, be always on the lookout for new opportunities. Follow through on things even if you cannot see the end clearly in sight.

Unexpected opportunities can come from left field. You can take advantage of these opportunities by putting yourself out there, following through on commitments, taking risks, meeting new people, and doing new things.

Something else the entrepreneur and those with dynamic mindsets have in common is their flexibility. They are open to constant change and improvement. People with these mindsets are ready to adapt and change plans.

Set your goals with specific outcomes. Know going in, there may be many changes to the plan before you get to your final destination. Be good with that. In fact, embrace it.

I've always been a nonconformist. Entrepreneurs aren't afraid to stand out and appear crazy to others. My daughters dislike it when I seem crazy, but that's okay. One day they'll get me!

Entrepreneurs embrace uniqueness and the qualities that make them different like badges, with pride. One of the many benefits is they differentiate themselves from their competitors. And, they create a more enjoyable and valuable experience for their clients.

People with an entrepreneur mindset set goals as a way to push themselves forward. The static mindset will tell you the goal is impossible to achieve and not worth the effort. If you're hearing this mental DJ, reframe it so you can look forward to reaching your desired outcome.

Finally, entrepreneurs surround themselves with other entrepreneurs, positive influences, and like-minded souls. They do this while networking, for motivation, and to find mentors with whom they can study and learn.

As you heard me talk about qualities of the entrepreneur mindset, where did you find yourself in that conversation? Did you feel many of them applied to you? Could you recognize areas where you can change or improve?

3 Steps to Reaching Your Goals

Just as you can cultivate a dynamic mindset, you can nurture the entrepreneur mindset in much the same way. With an entrepreneur mindset, you'll reach your goals.

Step 1: Recognize Your Mental DJ. Identify those thoughts you have that interfere with the qualities of an entrepreneur mindset. Learn to understand where those ideas originate.

You've now learned to reframe your thoughts. Also, you can use the magic trick of imagining you're talking to a friend rather than yourself.

This is challenging for many people at first. Keep practicing this method. Soon, you'll naturally reframe what you're saying to make it suitable advice for a friend.

Step 2: Release Your Entrepreneur Mindset. One of the best ways to expand your entrepreneur mindset is for you to connect with other entrepreneurs who have many of the mindset characteristics you want to nurture.

Attend conferences, seminars, and networking events. Search online for opportunities to get together with other high-achieving and like-minded entrepreneurs.

Join a mastermind group and learn from coaches who've already "been there and done that". They can help you achieve your goals much faster and more efficiently.

By actually getting out there and acting like an entrepreneur, you'll provide yourself with challenges and learning opportunities that will transform your life.

Earlier in this book, you thought of some qualities about your ideal life. Now let's look at your business. Organize some goals for your business. These goals could be things like grow your business in new markets, or increase revenue by twenty percent by hiring a virtual assistant to free up time so you can make more sales.

As you do this, listen to your mental DJ. Close your eyes and think through the goals you've identified. Write them down. By now, you should have a clear idea of where your limiting thoughts originate, and you can break down the source of each thought.

Step 3: Activate Your Goals. Take on an entrepreneur mindset. Take action. From your goals, you've now exposed your limiting thoughts, found the origin, and reframed them. Now, write down actions you can take to get you to where you need to go and continue to develop and grow.

Look, I know this personal mindset stuff isn't fun for everyone. I thank and congratulate you for doing this work. It's fundamental and has the power to change your life. Not just in business, but your personal life as well.

Get out there and have some fun with your new dynamic and entrepreneur mindsets. Think of them as muscles. The more you use them, the stronger they get.

CHAPTER TWO: CLIENT MINDSET

How do you provide such a valuable and enjoyable customer experience to turn each of your clients into a loyal, lifelong advocate and fan?

You do it by understanding the mindset of your perfect client. You do it by maximizing the entire customer experience from beginning to end. We aren't just talking about having excellent customer service, although that's part of it.

Your new customer experience begins when they first experience your brand. We'll examine and improve your entire client experience from start to... well, it never really finishes, it's ongoing.

Let's go deep into the mindset of your client and create the ultimate experience. After all, the experience of doing business with your brand is what you're selling. We aren't selling products and services, widgets, and tools, we're selling an experience. The entire experience at every level is essential.

Like everything else in life, all experience occurs in a person's mind. Different people will perceive experiences in different ways. That's why it's important we get into the mindset of your perfect client to develop the right experience for them.

We need to consider the client experience through the eyes of your client and manage that experience and make sure it's valuable and enjoyable.

In this chapter, we'll examine and fine-tune the customer experience for your business. Once complete, you'll have a detailed understanding of the client experience you offer and ways you can improve and streamline it.

Understanding and maximizing the client experience separates average companies from those that build strong, loyal relationships with their clients.

Sell the Experience

To be client centric, remove the mindset of selling products and services. Rather, sell the experience of doing business with your brand.

Let's start by defining what is meant by the customer experience. To get a good grasp on this somewhat difficult concept, let's look at the definition according to Wikipedia:

"Customer experience (CX) is the product of an interaction between an organization and a customer over the duration of their relationship."

The client experience that you provide, the interaction as Wikipedia describes it, includes that person's entire experience.

This experience encompasses the attraction, awareness, discovery, cultivation, advocacy stage, as well as the client making a purchase and consuming your product or service.

The customer experience can be measured by comparing the customer expectation across all the client touch points with the client's expectations.

To summarize: Your client's experience is much more than a regular interaction based on one transaction. It's that person's journey with you and your brand from beginning to end.

Oh, by the way, I should now distinguish between customer and client. You'll typically see me refer to a person who does business with you as either a person, an individual, or a client.

Even if you're selling widgets online, considering someone as a client, versus a customer, moves you towards thinking about repeat transactions with another person. A client is someone with whom you develop an ongoing relationship.

Some business people tend to consider a customer to be an entity worth a single transaction. Thinking about people as a client rather than a customer, we condition our mind for long-term relationships. We position our business for repeat sales.

So, while I do use the word customer, in most cases it's best to think in terms of client.

In a similar vein, let me share my thinking on the words business, company, and brand. We're all sales people regardless of what we do for a living. We are each our own brand, representing the brand of our company or business.

In most cases, I refer to a professional, company, or business as a brand. I suggest you do the same. Always think about the brand you represent and the value of your brand. We'll get into this more as we progress through this book.

Okay, back to the client experience. It includes the entire interaction your client has with your brand. This includes what happens not only externally, but deep within the inner thoughts and feelings of your client.

This experience includes both direct interactions and indirect experiences. This also involves how, when, and what your clients hear about your brand.

Some of what is experienced by your client isn't in your direct control. This means, within the aspects you control, you need to do everything you can to create that right experience for your client.

It's important for you to realize that all experience occurs in your mind. This mental function includes the point of view of every one of your individual clients. You need to get inside the head of the avatar, the persona, and the psychographic characteristics of your ideal client.

By creating an amazing experience for your clients, you'll turn them into loyal advocates for you and your brand.

The client experience is the big picture of your entire relationship with each person.

When people increase their investment in understanding and managing the client experience, they see higher rates of referral and satisfaction.

When you provide an amazing client experience, you'll find getting better clients will be easier for you. Your client base will become more loyal, they will refer you more, and your retention rates will skyrocket.

Your client experience will be amazing, exceeding their expectations. This amazing customer experience will keep them coming back to you for more.

It also keeps your clients from going to one of your competitors to get their needs met. People like to buy where they feel wanted. This is all about their mindset and associated with their feelings and psychology.

The client experience you're now creating will give you an advantage over your competitors. There's tremendous value to your clients for them to enjoy their experience while interacting with you.

Once you form this strong bond with your clients, you'll have no problem running your business on your terms. Your clients will treasure their relationship with you.

The client experience you provide helps differentiate you from your competitors. It has the power to render your competition irrelevant.

We'll need feedback to put this all together. You can get analytics and sales data to develop winning strategies, but there's nothing more effective than direct feedback from your clients themselves.

The good news is, few if any of your competitors do this work right now. Research indicates only around twenty percent of companies have a well-developed client experience strategy. This work you're doing gives you a huge advantage over eighty percent of everyone else, and is simple to put in place. I also think you'll find it fun to manage and maintain this area of your business.

An amazing client experience is where you exceed your client's expectations. A negative client experience happens when something falls short of expectations.

You cannot take shortcuts with client experience. You can damage your long-term relationships with your clients with just one bad experience, just one negative interaction.

It's human nature for people to share their negative feelings with others. Studies show that unpleasant experiences are shared more often than pleasant ones. This reinforces how important it is to always be client centric and provide an amazing customer experience.

Most of us have high expectations when we do business with someone. When those expectations aren't met, or worse yet, perceived, damage is done and not handled in a fair and proper way, then everything you did to build that relationship can go out the door.

Now, if you built up a ton of goodwill over time by providing amazing experiences and you mess up once, a client will likely let it go and stay with you. If you've done a great job in building that relationship, they may even share their feelings with you, which would be great. This might not be the case with other clients, such as those that are newer, or ones with whom you don't yet have a strong relationship.

When I was seventeen years old, I started a toy business, providing wrapped gifts for company Christmas parties. I built and operated this business for fifteen years and then sold the company.

I'll never forget the year I felt like the *Grinch Who Stole Christmas*. It was somewhere around year ten of my toy company, and I messed up with a client who had been with me from near the beginning.

It was one of my larger orders of several hundred toys, and I totally missed sending their order to them on the morning of their staff holiday party. The children at the party expected Santa to give them their annual gift, but none arrived that day. Somehow, I missed adding them to the right truck delivery schedule.

When I showed up to check in at the warehouse the following Monday, there was a huge pile of boxes sitting there that should've been delivered.

And, of course, an angry message was on my answering machine. Yes, I'm that old. We used a machine to receive phone messages. Weird as that may seem!

We shipped the toys out right away, and I brought a bottle of scotch over to Jim. He could tell how sorry I was and remained a loyal client to the end.

Of course, It wasn't the bottle of scotch or my apology that kept Jim on my side. Rather, it was the years of goodwill that preceded that unfortunate mistake.

I'm not sure I would've been as forgiving as Jim, so it was a lesson for me on many levels. This mishap contributed to my personal obsession with creating systems and being diligent in all aspects of my brand.

Even if someone doesn't experience disappointment with your brand, any negative press they discover can hurt your relationship. If they hear something third-hand or read a negative comment or review online, whether it's true or not, there's still the risk of your reputation being damaged. This negative press can put a dent in that client experience you worked so hard to put in place.

Negative experiences can spiral out of control, and you may not even realize the damage to your business. There are certain review sites out there, and new ones popping up all the time, with the sole purpose of creating negative reviews. The authors of these negative reviews then extort businesses who pay to have the negative reviews removed.

Of course, if there's something negative written about you or your company, it's not necessarily true. It just means someone, and maybe not even a client, perhaps a supplier or an employee, felt compelled to go online to one of these sites and air their grievance. It could even be a competitor seeking to cause you damage.

Be vigilant in this area. In our new economy with social media and online predators, it's easy for someone to take a misunderstanding or minor issue and blow it out of proportion. More than any time in history, it's essential you focus on that positive overall experience with everyone coming in contact with your brand.

4 Key Client Experience (CX) Stages

You now have a better understanding of its importance, and ramifications of the client experience and how it impacts your business. Now, let's look at some of the key stages of contact with your clients.

Discovery Stage: This is when someone first learns about you and your brand. It's that moment when you first come across his or her radar. This exposure could be through your advertising and marketing, online content, recommendations from a friend, or any number of other ways.

Remember, the point of this book is to teach you how to provide an amazing customer experience. That's my mindset. It comes across in my language, the way I look at things, and how I think about things. I want that same mindset to work for you too.

Interest Stage: People move from simple awareness of your brand to active engagement, seeking more information. They may research your company, look at your website, search online for your name, or ask a friend what they know about you.

Assuming all goes well, your process has primed that person for a taste of what you offer. This sampling could be a free trial, free content, or an opportunity to interact with you online or in person.

Relationship Stage: If you're providing financial services, this is where they transfer their portfolios to you. If you're a real estate salesperson, they list their homes with you. If you're a coach, an entertainer, or speaker, this is when they buy your product or engage your services. If you're a dog trainer, a plastic surgeon, an optometrist, or a chiropractor, they book appointments to see you.

Engaging your business, whether purchasing a service or a product, has a lot to do with you and the personality of your brand. It has everything to do with your, and your client's mindset.

After investing in your brand by consuming your product or service, your clients will experience some form of satisfaction. You'll meet the client's expectations, or you'll have disappointed them. Better yet, you'll have blown them away. The amazement just kicked in.

Follow-Up Stage: The post-purchase stage includes those things that happen after the initial buying decision. At this point, maybe you'll contact the client to provide more content, information, or offers, or request feedback from them. The repeat purchase stage is also an extension of this post-purchase stage.

Your client referral process is a crucial and often overlooked follow-up stage. This phase is when people will tell others about you, share your content, talk about you on social media, and spread the good word about you and your business. This is where they'll share their positive experience with others.

Think about the customer experience stages I just described. Think about how they relate to your business. It's important to focus on each additional client stage with at least as much attention as you give the initial stage. Of course, these stages can be broken down much further.

All Business is Show Business

Think about the current client experience your business delivers.

Approach this as if you're creating a story of your client's experience. In this story, the main character is your client.

As with all story development, we need to know the ins and outs of the characters. Define this person, your ideal client. Outline some of their key characteristics including their goals, needs, and desires.

Consider individual features of the persona of your ideal client. The easiest way for you to do this is to think of one particular person you do business with whom you enjoy. Make a note of some of their personality traits, their likes, and dislikes. If several people come to mind, think about whether most of them are men or women, and their age range. Identify what makes this person tick. What makes them a good client for you?

Previously, we identified different stages your client goes through as they experience you and your business. They were discovery, interest, relationship, and the follow-up stage.

These stages are appropriate for most businesses, but go ahead now and change them for your business if you feel you don't fit exactly into that mold.

Put yourself in the shoes of your client and consider what stages they go through with you and your company.

Note what you feel would make an enjoyable experience for your particular client. Think about, or better yet, write down what your expectations would be and what would amaze you.

It's crucial your client has an amazing experience at every stage. It's imperative you identify every touch point you have with your client to examine it and make sure it exceeds all their expectations.

Remember, at any given contact point, a bad experience, or an experience that falls short of expectations can be disastrous to your brand.

Think about what the experience is in each of these stages and how you can make them more fun and relevant to your client.

Your business should model show business. Meaning, the experience should entertain at some level. By adding an element of fun and personality into the experience of doing business with you, the client will enjoy interacting with your brand much more.

You can be amazing in subtle ways. For example, there are many methods to make your website interactive. Recently on my site to promote my corporate presentations, we made a small change with a huge impact. I added a choice of type of performance the client was looking for and placed check boxes for them to select. Within twenty-four hours, this one change resulted in my conversion rate nearly doubling.

This means every person who comes to my website now is twice as likely to fill out the form to inquire about booking one of my shows for their event. The only change I made was creating the ability for visitors to interact with the site in an easily understood and intuitive way, such as checking a box on the web page.

Notice this has nothing to do with being silly or funny. So, if you're a serious business, like a plastic surgeon or the equipment you sell is perceived as boring, you can still make the client experience interactive. Offering various forms of interaction is just one of many ways to add some show into your business. Interaction invokes emotion and enhances experience.

There are many client touch points where you can emulate show business to enhance your customer experience. These may be a website, print, or online advertising, and other key contact points with your client. Actively engage with these touch points and make sure they are as entertaining and interactive as possible for your client.

Disrupt their attention. Involve them and present opportunities to take action within your marketing channels.

If part of your business message is to educate, remember when you entertain people, they'll pay more attention. It will be easier for them to grasp your message. It will stick in their mind. Make the learning experience something they'll enjoy as you talk to them, so they'll remember like they remember their favorite television program, movie, or song.

When someone refers you to a potential client, this is a touch point. Any content you have with others through networking is also a touch point. This includes networking events and informal networking and online networking.

Just like networking and meeting people in person at conferences, if you have an office or store, this is a crucial touch point. Even if you do most of your business online, some of the most moving experiences your clients will have with you and your brand will be when you meet them in person.

Social media can come into play as a touch point for everything from the initial discovery stage, where your client first knows of you, through maintaining relationships. A solid social media strategy is crucial to your business in this new economy. Consider your current social media presence and the experience you offer your prospects and clients.

Your messages affect your client's experience. This includes your overall design, logos, language used in ad copy and on your website. It's all part of your show!

Look at everything from your client's perspective. Make sure to use colors your client would be comfortable with and enjoy seeing.

For example, if you're a financial professional, consider the use of blue which instills trust, maybe green or gold which implies wealth. These may seem like subtle distinctions, yet will affect your client in a profound way at a subconscious level.

When you relate on an emotional level with your client, their experience will be more meaningful for them, and they'll be more attracted to do business with you.

As a customer, whether it's eating at a restaurant or checking in with your dentist, your experience as a client has everything to do with your interaction with the waiter or the receptionist.

If you have employees or people who interact with your clients, whether it's in person or providing online or telephone support, provide proper training. Doing so will enhance your corporate culture and deliver a positive client experience. Your people are integral to your brand. You need to spend extra time in this area to lay out and systemize how they'll represent your business. Consistent messaging is key to success. Train your supporting cast.

While you would think search engine optimization (SEO) is only a topic for marketing, it's important to realize it also impacts your client experience.

Optimizing your website and your online marketing to correspond with keyword search terms submitted by your clients will make your site more popular with search engines. This visibility carries forward to play a role during many of the touch points going forward.

Perhaps, for example, someone forgets your website address so conducts a search for you online. Instead of you dominating the search result, your competitor does. Alternatively, worse yet, damaging results rank higher than your true representation.

Even if you have positive feedback online regarding you and your company, failure to show up in web searches can damage trust with your client.

The social proof you offer, whether testimonials, references, or other forms, is critical in setting up client expectations. When someone receives certain results from your product or service, others expect to receive the same results. People will trust the word of others more so than anything you provide or say about yourself.

Your brand reputation, third-party reviews, mentions in blogs, and social media comments all play a significant part in establishing your reputation. A positive or negative reputation contributes indirectly as an aspect of the client experience you're providing. Even when your clients or prospects trust you, negative mentions or comments can result in doubts in their mind.

Public relations or PR includes third-party mentions in official media like television or news articles. I'm not talking about paid advertisements or client reviews, but write-ups or stories in mass media.

Every step of your sales process offers a touch point. These are opportunities for showing your commitment to your client service and your consistency in the experience you provide.

Many people are more sensitive and conscious during the sales process touch point. This is when they're asked to part with their hard-earned money or offer you their trust to take care of their best interest.

You should always provide a trial offer or a no-commitment sample of your product or services. These include things like the free content you can give away as the enticement for someone to enter a relationship with you.

Offer something free, by way of content or consultation. If you're a dog trainer, you can provide a free video or instructions on how to teach your dog to sit. If you're a chiropractor, you might provide a free chiropractic treatment. If you're a financial advisor, you can offer a free consultation. If you sell cars or tractors, go for a test drive and throw the keys to the potential new owner for the weekend. These enticements apply to the touch point where you provide a no-risk sample of what you can offer to your potential customer. It's like a movie trailer.

Giving something for free is entrenched in the new economy, and if you aren't doing this now, you need to. Remember the experience is what they are buying from you so make it amazing, and they'll want more.

Whenever you follow up with your clients, whether it's a thank you or maybe another offer, give them a gift. Also, be sure to reciprocate when asking for a referral, testimonial, or review.

When you're delivering your product or service, whether in person or online or packaging sent in the mail, remember this is an important area concerning client satisfaction.

Delivery of the actual product or service is something often overlooked, yet it's so important not to mess it up. Think of my earlier example when I talked about being served by a waiter or greeted by a receptionist, this is part of the delivery of that service.

A restaurant owner relies on her service staff to deliver a product consistent with the overall experience promoted.

This same principle of remaining congruent with service applies to all after-purchase support to help someone to consume a product or service. This includes refunds, complaints, returns, or any other support you offer. These are important touch points, and they must be aligned with your brand.

Are you running any incentive or loyalty programs? If you offer these kinds of programs to your clients, this is yet another way people experience your service.

Moreover, all communication with your clients, from the beginning of the awareness stage to the ongoing purchase stage, and the follow-up stage, again are all significant touch points.

The next important area for us to delve into is identifying various communication channels between you and your client. These include all the ways you communicate. Write them all down and be as accurate as possible.

Don't use general terms like the internet, advertising, or social media. Rather, identify specific websites, blogs, forums, advertising media, social media sites, and so on. Be specific.

Consider time-sensitive areas which include delivery times, follow-up, communication with your client, showing up at appointments, and whatever else you can think of relating to your particular situation.

You can also add specific amounts of time where you have actual data, such as the time it takes from the initial contact with your company to the first purchase. Timeframes are a major factor in your client experience. If there are areas where your services take too long, you'll need to focus and improve. Like comedy, it's all about timing.

As we examine the mindset of your client, it's critical you pinpoint specific moments during each process where your client may experience emotions or moments of truth. These might be moments like the feeling of satisfaction at first using your product or service. Or, it may be when the client realizes your offering is unique and distinct to them.

One way to find this out is to survey them. You can also have people close to you who also fit your ideal client avatar experience your products. Have them tell you when they felt emotion related to their experience in doing business with you. These valuable insights will make a world of difference in your (show) business.

Your customer experience begins at the earliest stages of your client's awareness of your brand and leads to them becoming lifelong, raving fans of you and your business.

How to Create an Amazing CX

The key to branding is consistency. Your client experience must be consistent from beginning to end. Achieving this consistency begins with you defining your brand.

Plan to make every touch point, every interaction, and all other parts of your client's experience consistent with your brand.

The way to do this is by identifying and communicating your core values. Your core values will include such things as how you want people to feel and the relationship you desire to have with your clients. It will also include how you want your clients to speak about you and describe their experience with you and your business. All of this, and a lot more, drives what you do to create that ideal client experience.

It starts with you and your core values. Most of what others teach about branding and identifying your ideal client is backwards.

You may be aware that pinpointing who your client is, and creating an avatar for them, is a great place to start when fine-tuning your brand identity. In fact, we have done that already in this book and will do more of it, as it's important.

However, your avatar, who you are, and your core values come first. If they aren't in line with the avatar of your client, then your client won't be attracted to you. So, it's easier and makes more sense for you to look at you and what you stand for and build your client experience outward from there.

Here's where this becomes practical advice right now. If you don't feel you're in the right line of work and serving people who are your best target market, it's time to make a change. Rather than trying to adapt to them, look at who you are and what you stand for. Then determine what it is you can offer to a particular group of people. Build your business based on what you value and what you're passionate about.

Okay, let's get back to identifying your core values. This includes how you want people to feel, what type of relationship you want to have with your clients, and what you want them to say about you. All of this drive what you do to create the ideal client experience.

Remember, you need to communicate your core values to your clients.

The client experience is the relationship between you and your client. You must identify what kind of relationship this is. Ask yourself about the relationship to better understand it. Make a point of including emotions you want to evoke in your client's mind. Also, consider the culture of your organization you want to convey to your clients. This includes your company's personality, and how your clients perceive it.

Even though it's best to start with you, and let the ideal client be attracted to you, still pay close attention to your client's persona.

Knowing your client's likes and dislikes is crucial in creating an amazing customer experience. You need a deep understanding of your client and a realization that nothing matters more than how they experience doing business with you.

This is how you go about designing your amazing customer experience. With a thorough understanding of their needs and goals, their motivations, what makes them tick, and why they behave in certain ways, you have the foundation to support your amazing customer experience.

Use real client data to get these insights. Survey your clients, even if it's just asking how they feel. Although, there are much more systematic ways of doing it.

The more you personalize the experience and make it feel like a relationship, the more loyalty you'll develop.

Most people I speak with about brand positioning look at branding in broad brush strokes. They overlook the many small factors that contribute to the brand image in the mind of the client.

True branding factors affecting your client's relationship include your choice of graphics, fonts, and colors. It also includes your appearance, how you dress, and how your breath smells.

However, it's also transmitted by your supporting cast, such as your employees. Your receptionist, your message on your voicemail, all of these are important. Don't overlook even the smallest factor. People at some level, whether conscious or unconscious, get to know you and form an impression of you from all the little things. All the little things create the big picture for them about who you are and whether they can trust you. They'll use this information to decide whether to employ your brand or not.

While we're still dealing with the client mindset, we need to touch on those unique elements specific to you and your company. What sets you apart from everyone else? Specific elements here are critical in the overall client experience. Most likely, it's these things that your clients value the most about you. These are the reasons a person doesn't go to your competitor, or even look around for someone else.

Be clear on your unique value proposition to your client. How are you different from all others in your market?

Take a deep breath in through your nose, hold for three seconds, and release your breath steadily out your mouth.

Why are you unique? Without giving it analytical thought, say aloud right now the first thing that comes to mind. What is this statement, and what unique benefits will it convey to your client about your brand?

This statement will show them, in words, what you do and how you do it, and that it differs from your competitors. It's that unique quality about the experience you provide which is the reason a person buys from you. It's your promise, your commitment to your client.

Make a note of that statement. This unique differentiator is how you attract better clients and bigger sales.

The best way for you to discover what's unique about you, if you didn't know right away, and even if you do, is to ask your clients.

So often in life, the view we have of ourselves differs from those of people around us. We learned this when we delved into our own mindset in the last chapter. Find time to double check your view of yourself by getting input from others. This will be time well invested.

Instead of determining your unique value proposition solely on your own, get feedback. The feedback you receive will help you better understand what others are thinking. This allows you to make sure your unique value proposition is of value to your clients.

As we focus on the client experience, it's important to realize it goes far beyond the logical or physical attributes of your product or service.

A well-designed and executed customer experience will trigger emotions in your clients. The feelings that affect them will allow them to connect to your brand and will lead to their retention and loyalty.

An amazing client experience stirs up emotions. This builds a bond between you and your client, inspiring loyalty as you deliver an amazing experience.

The moments that create this experience don't have to be monumental or earth shattering. In fact, it's the small things, the simple things, which make a huge difference.

Let me give you some examples. I'll risk appearing like a tough customer as I share one of my pet peeves and tell you how I would do things differently.

I eat at restaurants a lot. Not only because I travel, but no one in my house, including myself, likes to cook.

There's something that bothers me at restaurants, and it seems to happen all the time. I'll be in the middle of chewing my food, and the waiter will come up and ask me "How are those first bites?" Now, I don't know about you, but I was taught it's rude to talk with my mouth full. It's also rude to ignore people when they're talking to you.

If I managed a restaurant, I would train my staff not to approach a table when the guests have food in their mouths. Rather, while the guests aren't chewing on food, approach, and ask how everything is.

Now, with a big table, it might be hard for the waiter to time a visit when no one is in the middle of munching down their salad. Then, at least direct the question to someone who isn't eating.

Here's another example of what a restaurant can do to improve the client experience. Provide a basket at the table where patrons can store their bags and accessories, rather than placing them on the table or floor. I've never seen this done. It's a simple thing, and not a big deal. A thoughtful gesture such as this provides a unique value and an amazing experience for the customers.

For someone in the service business working with high-value clients, there are so many ways to deliver an amazing customer experience.

You need to know what will delight your particular client. You must anticipate their wants and desires, and deliver value to them before they even ask.

Personalize your service and pay particular attention to the small details. Give this some thought and put yourself in your client's shoes. Think about how you can exceed your client's expectations in many small ways.

Brands to Model

Here are three examples of major brands that do this better than others. Their ability to deliver an exceptional customer service experience is a big part of what makes them a major brand.

Jeff Bezos, the CEO of Amazon, has always stated that everything his company does is completely client centric. Amazon made itself the world's biggest online retailer by doing just that. Amazon made sure the experience of shopping at Amazon revolves around the consumer. The peer-to-peer reviews and client communities have put us, the clients, in charge and give us a place to share our interests with others.

Amazon is an e-commerce giant today. In part, because of the great terms of service, guarantees, convenience, reliability, website friendliness, and fair pricing. At every step in your experience with Amazon, you feel it's about you.

You expect an excellent experience, and that's what you get.

Recently, I was thinking about how I can offer the best possible experience to my audience at a corporate show. I looked to Amazon to get some ideas to customize a hypnosis show for fifteen hundred doctors.

In searching Amazon for medical products, I brainstormed some ideas for the show. One idea was to have a group of the audience hypnotized on stage, then suggest to one person to go back to her seat and hand out gloves to everyone in the audience as if they were preparing for an emergency. Of course, the hypnotized audience member will think it's an emergency she's preparing for. She will frantically hand out the gloves to the laughing audience members and stress how important it is the gloves are worn when dealing with the emergency situation.

Another idea is to give the suggestion for someone to take off his shirt and put on some scrubs every time I say the word "scrubs." Someone else could be given a stethoscope and at first, have no idea what it's for. Later, the stethoscope-wielding doctor will run through the audience to check everyone's heart rate.

I spent less than a hundred dollars buying the stethoscope, rubber gloves, scrubs, and a few other items to use as props and give away during the show.

The cost was minimal. The source of inspiration was vast. It was convenient to order these items and prepare for the show. I enjoyed an excellent client experience on the Amazon website, while I focused on providing an amazing experience for my clients.

There wasn't any conversation with my booking agent on tailoring the performance, and no extra fee to the client to do so. It's my duty to make my show as memorable as possible. This extra effort is part of my branding. This is just one small example of how I'm client centric. By adding unique value, my show is no longer a commodity. That's one reason I'm booked year after year by the same clients at fees reflective of my value.

One more thing I noticed is how Amazon makes it easy to buy these same products again. I may do that if I have another show at another time for a group of doctors. I appreciate Amazon for anticipating my potential need to reorder these same items.

IKEA is another company that knows its clients well. They realize home furnishings aren't just about functionality and price. It's also about expressing yourself, or, in effect, creating your brand for your home.

The user experience on the website and at their locations makes it easy to buy from them. IKEA has connected with their clients through an online community. These fans share project ideas with each other and ask each other for suggestions and feedback. Through this online community, IKEA clients discuss artistic ideas for home decorating and get feedback from other like-minded people.

It's evident when doing business with IKEA and Amazon they value you as a client and a human being.

They have anticipated your needs and desires. Your experience dealing with them is enjoyable, and many people want to share this experience with others.

Apple and Starbucks are other brands to model. As are Uber, Netflix, Chipotle, and Virgin America.

Can you learn from these examples? What can you apply to your business? It doesn't matter how small or large your business is. An amazing client experience is achievable for all of us. What does your brand promise? How do you amaze people?

Think about and list the top three core values of your business. Consider the emotions you want your clients to feel. List three or four of these emotions.

Write down the type of relationship you want to have with your clients. What is appropriate and most comfortable for you? What would be most suitable for your client?

Finally, write out some statements you want your clients to say about their experience with your brand. Imagine how they react after interacting with you. What would they say about you when they are on the phone with a friend?

If the conversation isn't how you would like it to be, don't worry. We'll keep working through this and create the experience that will provide the outcome you want to achieve.

How to Integrate Your Brand and CX

Always be client centric. Keep in mind your client's persona, your target market, your brand, your unique value proposition, and your core values.

Consider the big picture. Go beyond you, your business, and your client interactions. Consider the entire client experience, which includes your core values, who you are, what you stand for, and every aspect of your brand.

Look for areas in your business that are behind the scenes. These are areas where you may not have direct contact with your clients. This unseen activity can affect your client experience. Make sure it reflects your brand and your core values.

Also, be mindful of the material you publish. The content and presentation need to reflect your brand and core values. It plays a significant role in forming the overall experience people have with your brand.

Everything you do must support your brand. It all contributes to what you and your company are all about. Any content you publish will affect your client's experience. Content such as your website, blog posts, or articles. Also, content that includes social media posts, videos, information pamphlets, infographics, or podcasts. And the content of courses, teleseminars, or webinars. All this content will have an impact on your client's experience. Always stay on brand.

Double check the guidelines and standards you have in place. Make sure you draft them with the client experience in mind. Consider how each policy, whether written or not, affects the client experience. Take the time to consider this for each guideline and standard.

I'm talking about everything you do. Evaluate the fonts and images you use in documents. Evaluate your online presence. Evaluate the quality standards for your products. Evaluate your business practices and procedures. Evaluate how you follow up and provide service.

Do you have processes and systems in place in your business?

I hope so. If not, now is the time to do something about it. While it's not the primary subject of this book, I encourage you to look at what you do on a routine and repetitive basis. Systemize or automate these processes and activities.

The operating procedures of your company, your business, and your brand have a significant impact on your customer's experience. You need to set them up with the client in mind.

As with your guidelines and standards, pay attention to any processes and systems that don't deal directly with your clients. They can have an impact. These are items like accounting, IT policies, protocols for meetings, web traffic analysis, and so on. These business practices can impact your company culture, which ultimately affects your client.

Even if you're a one-person service provider, like a coach, consultant, advisor, or a practitioner, you still must manage your company culture. No matter how small your organization, you have a company culture. You have a brand to support this culture. Your brand and your culture will be felt by your clients, either directly or indirectly.

If you have staff, such as salespeople or other employees, lack of training is an indirect way of telling them you don't value them. Worse, it also means you don't value your clients. Not providing training is careless, and will lead to low morale among staff and translate into poor customer service.

As consumers, clients, or patients, you and I have experienced this time and time again. How often have you gone into a store and been treated poorly by a salesperson and thought to yourself they must be treated poorly by the business?

Offering training to your staff sends a strong message you care about your brand and your clients. Though being friendly and kind are common courtesies, training your staff about your brand and core values is more powerful. Train your staff. Show respect to your clients.

Training covers topics such as understanding your products, your service offerings, your brand, and your core values.

As a financial professional, are you up to speed on all the latest products you can offer your clients?

As a medical professional, are you knowledgeable about the latest treatments?

If you're a speaker, a coach, or entertainer, are you staying current and being cutting edge and innovative?

Depending on your business, different types of training will be more important than others. Always keep learning. Share your knowledge with the people who support your brand.

How's your communication with your clients as it relates to your brand voice style? How aggressive or passive is your communication when you're selling and providing service to your clients?

Think about communication channels you use and the extent to which your communications are promotional versus informative. Examine the use of scripts if you use them. If you don't use scripts, consider the value they add when it's critical you get important details across to your clients.

How you communicate both within your company and with the public have a major influence on your clients.

Internal communications are necessary for establishing your business culture and also ensuring productivity. For example, if you communicate quickly with your different departments to answer a client's question, they can provide faster service to your client.

What to consider about client communication include style (how assertive or passive), distribution channels, and the extent to which messages are promotional. Specific communication protocols (or scripts) should be deployed.

Many people involved with you and your business in various capacities can have an influence on your client's experience. This includes employees, both those on the front lines and those behind the scenes, business associates, sponsors, brand advocates, and so on.

For example, even if you're in a service business, you may have some product involved in the fulfillment of your service. Perhaps you outsource the manufacturing of this product to a third-party company. The company's quality standards and business process will have a direct impact on the product's quality. The product's quality will directly affect how your clients experience your service.

If you have an affiliate program, everything your affiliates do affect the reputation of your brand. For this reason, I'm cautious when considering any joint venture, or affiliate relationship since I've had issues in the past.

Be diligent in who you select and keep associated with your business. They'll either help or hurt you. They'll either contribute in a positive way or harm your brand.

If there's any association you've been considering cutting loose, do yourself a favor. Make the change. Think about how important these relationships are to your business and your clients.

How to Avoid Breakdowns in Your CX

No matter what type of business you're in, you need to respond to inquiries and support requests quickly. A slow response to clients is one of the easiest ways to lose their trust and one of the primary reasons clients leave one company for another. It's easy to outperform your competition in this area since many businesses don't reply promptly. This is one easy way you can be amazing.

Make sure everyone on your team maintains a high level of friendliness and professionalism 100% of the time. The adage claiming the client is always right isn't always true. However, we must satisfy the needs of our clients. We need to help them understand what they need. This means you and your team must listen to your clients, hear what they're saying, and direct them to the best solution.

It can be disastrous if a client with a complaint can't get ahold of you or anyone else in your company promptly. Also, if a representative of your brand is rude, or perceived as being rude, significant problems can arise.

Even if your communication is civil and controlled, miscommunications can escalate small issues into a big deal.

Earlier in the book, we examined the potential pitfalls of a poor client experience and how that can end up online and damage your reputation whether you deserve it or not.

Providing excellent customer support, client service, and dealing with people in a fair manner is more important now than ever. When you care enough to deliver amazing service, you demonstrate you care about your client.

Make sure everybody on your team acutely knows the ramifications of miscommunication or losing their cool with a client. Whether the customer is a jerk or not, don't lose your cool. Especially if they're a jerk since they cause the most damage, go out of your way to amaze them.

Make a list of the different types of communications you have with your clients and suppliers.

Communication methods include the telephone, texting, face-to-face contact in the office, one-on-one meetings, group meetings, Skype meetings, and email. Look at each method, and create systems and protocols to prevent any slip ups by you or others representing your brand. Do this to promote and protect your brand, and to deliver an amazing client experience.

Miscommunication and poor communication pose a real and direct threat to the health of your brand and business. I'm talking about things like attitude, body language, and facial expressions which can significantly impact an encounter.

Also, consider the use of ALL CAPITAL LETTERS in an email. This is yelling in an email and isn't professional. No one likes to be yelled at, not even in an email.

Poorly executed social communications, especially on public forums, can severely harm the perception others have of you and your brand. When someone asks a question, leaves a comment, or sends a message on social media, it's critical you respond quickly and professionally.

Let's say your client is unhappy with your online chat support service and they air their grievance on social media in front of their hundreds of followers. This negative review can be disastrous for you and your company's reputation. The damage can be mitigated if you act quickly. You can even turn it into an excellent opportunity to show how much you care. By responding quickly, addressing the client's needs and being professional, you show you care. You can turn these negative moments into positive ones that support your brand. Convert what might be a negative client experience into a positive one.

Using this as an example, one way to handle the situation would be to reply to the client with an apology and a request for clarification. Ask them to explain what happened and empathize with their need or concern. Deal with whatever grievance they have, and make it up to them. This can be shared with their friends on Facebook. Use this opportunity to be amazing.

This shows your client and their audience, though your company may not be perfect, you'll listen and improve because you highly value your clients.

It's up to you to monitor your brand. Diligently following your brand on social media and swiftly responding is crucial.

Some of this information may be obvious to you. You might think, of course, you would do these things and respond positively. You would take action to make things right. You want everything to be good. However, it's not sufficient just to be reminded of that right now. Or, to want to do these things. You need to have a plan, and you need to take action. Make lists of these different points and prepare in advance. Be diligent in your communication and follow the protocols which I'm suggesting.

Some automated systems are essential for a business to run smoothly. This is especially true when you experience a high volume of sales and other client interactions. However, some systems pose a huge risk because they may not work properly.

Always check your automated systems. Try them out by posing as a client. For example, use your online shopping cart and make a purchase. Make this a routine part of your business so you can correct any problems before clients experience them. Don't do this just once. Do this periodically to make sure your systems are working properly. Also, make sure you keep your automated systems updated.

For example, let's say you're communicating with your clients through an email list. Your autoresponder automates the process of sending out messages. However, suppose there's a mistake with the email message template you're using, and it addresses your recipients as something like "first name" instead of their actual name.

This email error is a minor mistake. Many recipients would shrug it off. But it shows you don't pay attention to detail. It could lead the client to ask, "What else do they do that's sloppy? Perhaps, the handling of my personal data?" This is a perception you need to avoid at all costs.

It's often hard to walk the fine line between promoting enough and over-promoting. While not promoting enough could mean your message is getting lost on your clients, over-promotion can have a negative impact on the client experience.

If you're using social media to communicate with your clients and all your messages are promotional, this could lead your followers to tune you out. They'll skip past your updates or block them. You'll look like a company that only communicates when it wants to sell something.

On the other hand, if you send out useful and interesting content, the kind of updates your clients look forward to, you'll be regarded as a trusted source of information and entertainment. Sharing information is a good way to personalize your brand and increases the likelihood people will buy from you.

When in doubt, err on the side of less promotion. Don't over-promote on social media or online forums. Try to let your content do the promoting for you, and only promote on media that's promotion friendly. This would be your website, a marketing brochure, or an advertisement. When in doubt, ask for a third-party opinion whether your promotion is tasteful or not.

With technology, so many things can go wrong. Maybe your website is slow to load. It may not be responsive, meaning it doesn't display well on smaller devices like a cell phone or tablet. If you use VOIP technology for your phones, make sure connections are clear and don't cut off frequently. Many clients will understand these things occur once in a while. Nevertheless, it affects their experience in dealing with you.

Do whatever you can to ensure the technological aspects of your business are up to date and running smoothly. Take a moment now and identify points in your client's experience where a technical failure could annoy or be disastrous. Make changes now to avoid any negative impact on your client.

Set up a regular maintenance schedule to check on your tech. Check things, for example, like the plug-ins you've installed if you're using WordPress. Plug-ins break or lose functionality. This usually happens when the WordPress software gets updated, and the plug-in doesn't. Keeping these functions up to date is essential to your client's experience.

Always remember, the client expects not to be let down. They expect a certain level of quality from you, your products, and your services. Meet this expectation and be consistent. Identify and fix anything that poses a risk to this consistency.

After making a sale, always follow up. This part of the client experience solidifies your relationship with the client. It shows them you're interested in building a solid relationship and not just looking for a one-time sale. Make sure you have some follow up in place, and that it's systemized and ongoing.

It may not always be obvious where breakdowns might occur during the client journey. You could identify some just from what you know about your business. Yet, a better way is to gather objective data telling you where and how it's happening.

Sources of data include surveys where you gather client feedback. This is a great way to find out if your clients are in any way unhappy with their experience. Doing this results in improving engagement with your clients, it gets them involved, and it shows them you truly care.

You can look at website analytics to shed light on things such as how people get to your site. Use tools like heat maps to discover the actions people take when on your site. Analytics will let you know what pages are visited and where they exit your website.

Preventing these breakdowns should be a regular part of your business operations, and there are several ways you can do this.

Make a note of the places where your current client experience is most at risk. Review every critical area for potential breakdowns. Conduct research if you're not sure of the current quality of these experiences. Mark down those areas that need immediate attention. List the actions you need to take to address them.

Note at least three steps you'll take to prevent potential breakdowns in the client's experience. Then, implement those actions.

By working through this chapter, you now have a great start in creating that amazing experience for your clients. Take the next steps and set deadlines for each of the things you need to do. This will give you a solid timeframe for getting them done.

Once you've created the best experience possible for your clients, you'll see better results from all your marketing activities.

I know you want to get to the marketing tactics and the latest sales methods. From my experience, that's where most people gravitate.

Most of your competitors won't have done this foundational work. That's why you'll stand out and win. This foundation is critical to the success of your sales and marketing efforts. It will give you an advantage over everyone else in your market.

PART TWO: MESSAGE

"Share your story, or others will make one up for you."

CHAPTER THREE: YOUR BRAND VOICE

How you express yourself when doing business is your brand voice. Your personality comes through in your writing, language, and tone.

With a distinct persona and brand identity, your uniqueness will shine through. Honing this is an opportunity for your brand to stand out from others. When your brand voice is distinct enough, your clients will recognize you even when no name or logo is visible.

A simple definition of brand voice is the style and tone of your communications. It conveys a consistent message about who you are to your audience. Your brand voice sets your business apart from others, regardless of your market niche. Brand voice conveys your business identity.

The words you use when you speak to your clients and the sentences you write are what determine your brand's voice. Your words create a consistent persona in the minds of your audience. This happens whether you take control of your message or not. It's important for you to determine in advance the tone of your communication.

Most of what we work on in this chapter will be existing elements of you and your brand. We'll be proactive and smart by thinking this through, planning, and taking action.

You're committed to growing your business and always providing an amazing experience for your clients. This means there are many good reasons to determine and guide your voice.

When you create a consistent experience across your business touch points, you're creating a brand image. This experience you share is imperative. It tells your audience who you are. When done well, it sets up your foundation and maintenance of trust between you and your client.

By focusing on your brand voice, you create an image in your audience's mind. This image tells them who you are as a brand. It's a constant reminder of the experience they can expect from you.

When you create your brand voice, you're one step closer to eliminating your competition. Your unique brand voice cuts through the noise of other companies and individuals. When done well, you can make your competition vanish.

As a business owner, your unique brand voice will force you to make decisions at every step in your content creation workflow. By doing your groundwork now, you'll easily create compelling content recognizable as yours.

Your brand voice creates an emotional connection between you and your audience. This connection is established through your message, your words. You'll maintain this relationship through the content you produce and share. This emotional connection you create will inspire brand loyalty and encourage repeat business.

Finally, your brand voice can influence your clients, moving them closer to making a purchase. Your ability to influence increases when your clients become familiar and comfortable with your unique voice.

Your brand voice will come across in all areas of your marketing interactions with your clients. You broadcast your voice on your marketing content such as your website, social media, email campaigns, and all direct and indirect interaction with your clients.

To find examples of brands who have already thought this through, just search online for examples of brand voice. You'll find a lot of them. Some examples will relate more so than others to you and your business. This is a worthy exercise and a great way to get some new ideas.

Once you define your brand voice, you need to create guidelines to spell out how you portray this in your content. Make sure all your written material and visuals including print, posters, logos, and all other material, is consistent with your voice. These guidelines can be outlined in a chart format for easy reference.

Put this together, and you'll have a chart, not only for yourself but also for other representatives of your brand.

It's important you realize your brand voice isn't a logo, a headline, or tagline. Instead, it's your brand personality. Your brand voice isn't so much what you say, but rather how you share your message.

For example, in email correspondence, a casual way to address someone would be "Hey Barb, how ya doing?" The more formal version of that would be "Hello Barb, how are you?"

You can see how the more casual phrase conveys a particular personality. A more formal greeting conveys something else. Your voice will alter based on how familiar you are with the person you're addressing. I think you get the message.

You got it?

Do you understand?

Capiche?

Do you recognize my brand voice? It's slightly more formal in this book than in my videos, or when I conduct keynote speeches and seminars. But, it's still somewhat casual and reflects my personality.

Okay, so you understand the important benefits of developing your voice which will stand out and personify your business.

It begins with essential client research and looking at their core values.

Describe your brand personality and how that voice can differentiate you from your competition. This will help you attract better clients and make bigger sales.

For your brand voice, you need to define its style, tone, and language. Doing this in detail will allow your brand voice to be consistent when implemented by you and others.

Put guidelines together for your brand voice. This will ensure your voice is used in all your marketing content, and in all interactions with your business at every level.

Create a plan for implementation. This plan will be updated since your brand voice will evolve over time. Even though it will evolve and change, you can count on your brand voice retaining your core driving principles and personality.

Go ahead and make notes of the benefits and specific goals you have for creating your unique voice for your brand. Ask yourself how your brand voice will help you in your marketing, with your product development, and with other people who support you and your business.

List all the areas you think your brand voice can speak louder and clearer. Identify where you can better communicate to the client who you are and the essence of your personality.

Steps to Develop Your Brand Voice

Right now, we're dealing with the messaging of you and your business. This provides you with the foundation you need to craft your brand voice. It will also come in handy in all three parts of your business as we work on mindset, message, and marketing.

There are four steps for us to go through. These steps will allow you to develop and implement your unique and special brand voice.

By uncovering your brand personality and the strength that already lies within it, you create consistency in your marketing. Learning to embody that personality in the tone and words you use will help maintain relationships with your clients. By doing this, you'll stand out from your competitors.

Step One: You guessed it, step one is performing client research. Start by performing client research to understand their needs, motivations, points of pain, and triggers to purchase. Discover what motivates their purchase patterns, and how your products or services meet their needs.

Refer to any data you have that is related to your client demographics and purchases. Include information from other interactions from online channels, such as social media. Besides the data you collect based on client interactions, take advantage of surveys. Surveys are easy to run using email or website plug-ins that pop up for your site visitors to answer questions. Also, look at comments from blogs and social media. Review your client testimonials. Pay attention to what they like about your brand voice.

Whenever possible, seek in-person encounters with your clients. These yield the most authentic information and real-world examples of the language they use.

You'll collect information such as demographics which includes age, location, income level, gender, language, education level, and so on. Psychographic information which is information on specific personalities, attitudes, values, pain points, hobbies, future dreams, and hopes. Media consumption habits such as what magazines, TV shows, movies, websites, and apps your client likes to consume and utilize.

Review purchasing habit data. Look at data that helps you understand the purchasing behavior of your clients, and how they feel about the products they buy. Find out how they feel about spending money, and how they like the products and services delivered to them.

Step Two: In this step, you'll examine your competitor's data. Read their reviews, testimonials, and social media comments. If some of your clients are also clients of your competitors, it's a great advantage for you to see and understand how your clients feel about your competitors. As you begin to understand how your clients feel about your competitors, this will help you clarify your unique position in the market.

You're doing this so you can learn what's important to your clients. Pay close attention to the specific words and phrases they use. This will help you develop your vocabulary and tone of writing. This all helps you speak to your clients in their language.

Most likely, you'll find there are certain adjectives your clients use more often than others. For example, words like reliable, energy, fun, or consistent. Some words you learn will surprise you. This will change the way you communicate and deliver your products and services.

Step Three: Take the pieces of information you find useful, and prioritize them by importance and relevance to your goals. For example, if you try to position yourself as a brand that offers conservative advice, examine the data you've gathered where clients refer to conservative advice.

A client may say something like, "I don't expect way above average returns from Joe's financial advice, but it's always conservative, and this makes me feel safe. I'm comfortable with the peace of mind."

Step Four: Look at the big picture the data paints to define your client's personality, values, and buying needs. This will help you develop a brand voice your perfect client is attracted to.

To speak your client's language, you need to know this persona, and naturally and comfortably speak to it. The bottom line is you need to know who they are, what makes them tick, and how they like to be spoken to and treated.

This all comes back to you being client centric and do it in a way your best clients will enjoy and appreciate. All, while maintaining your core values and personality.

To further develop your ideal client avatar or persona, you need to ask and answer a variety of questions.

- What does he or she look like?

- What's important to them?

- What do they want from you and your brand?

- What common words and phrases do they use?

You'll end up with several personas within your target client base. This is the case for me and my business, and will be the same for you and most mature businesses.

Think of the major categories, the larger segments, and higher-value targeting of your client base. Create a specific avatar for just your most substantial groups. It's unnecessary right now for you to focus on the minor segments of your target market.

Earlier, we identified core values for you and your organization. Your clients expect your core values to show through in your voice.

Some examples of core values are your commitment to quality, your efforts to innovate, your accountability, and a high level of integrity and amazing client service.

These attributes help make up the experience you provide for your clients.

It's easy to get into abstract concepts when we're talking about core values. It's not good enough to say we always try to do the right thing. Strong core values need to be specific and sustainable, personable, and relevant.

Have a look at the way your business operates right now.

Ask yourself these questions:

- What are your core values?

- What are your strengths?

- What do your clients come to expect from you?

Your core business values are the foundation upon which you build your brand. It's important to define these clearly and accurately.

Choose the keywords or phrases that best describe your brand. This helps define your character or persona.

The language you use will reflect your core values. It will also communicate your values to your clients in a way that's easy for them to understand. For example, let's say you sell eco-friendly clothing. Your keywords or phrases should emphasize your product's eco-friendliness, sportiness, or durability. The images that speak to these qualities might include a picture of someone diving into a lake in a pine forest, or a group of children in the Amazon smiling and playing.

Brainstorm and list adjectives that describe who you are as a business, as a brand. Use adjectives as if your business were an actual person. One good way to brainstorm this is to think of words and phrases that describe how you want your clients to feel when they encounter you and your products or services.

For example, let's say you're a chiropractor and your keywords or phrases emphasize a healthy back, a straighter spine, pain relief, or physical mobility. The images that show these qualities might include a picture of someone doing yoga, standing tall, climbing a mountain, having fun, playing with their kids, and living a healthy lifestyle.

Once you've found images that reflect the feelings you want to create about your brand, you can then brainstorm adjectives that go with the pictures.

You have a large list of descriptive words from which to choose. A good way to narrow them down is to try out each one to see what images play out in your mind.

Look for the words or short phrases that sound like you and that also reflect the research you've done about your clients.

Which of the keywords or phrases most accurately reflect the feelings your clients report experiencing? Which ones reflect the way you want your clients to feel during their experience with your brand?

Keep narrowing down and prioritizing your list until you've identified the top three adjectives or short phrases which best express the most important feelings you want to elicit in your clients. These form the initial foundation for defining the specifics of your brand voice and identity.

Pick the top three words to define your brand personality.

Now you have a clear way of expressing your core values and personality to your clients. You need to make your brand unique enough so it will stand apart from your competitors.

Dig into the data and the ideas you collected. Find the distinct things that make your business different from others. Make a list that describes point by point your differences. This list supports your differentiating factors.

The research you did on your competitors will come in handy now. For each value or keyword, consider how you do this in ways different from your competitors. Incorporate this into your tone and language. This will let you cut through the noise of the other companies in the market targeting clients similar to yours.

This is how you'll stand out and render your competition irrelevant. You can make them disappear, like a magician!

Conduct your client research. Uncover what your clients say they like about you, your solution, or your product. Note the three things they want most.

Describe what your target client looks like, talks like, cares about, and what they believe. List what they like to read, where they shop, where they browse online, what they follow on social media or the news, and any other details you can find to describe them.

Note specific language and phrases your clients use. If you don't have this information, do research to find out. The best way is to talk with your best clients.

Describe the personality of your brand and list at least ten words or phrases to describe you and your business. Take those ten words or phrases and narrow them down to the top three to describe your brand personality.

If there are businesses within your niche that you dislike, then note what they do that turns you off. Then list the key points that make you different. Write down why you're so much better and how you provide a much more personalized and rewarding client experience.

Identify your brand's differentiating factors.

Make a list of other companies you believe you're most like.

Include companies you want to be like.

What do you admire about them?

How to Fine-Tune Your Brand Voice

So far, you've identified core values and specific adjectives, language, and differentiators that form the basis for your brand voice.

Now, you'll take these ideas and concepts and put them into practice and develop guidelines to create a consistent brand voice. The result is that no matter which member of your team communicates with your clients, the message will be the same.

The first thing you need to do is establish the tone of your brand's voice. This is how you want your content to sound to your audience. Is it scientific and formal, or friendly and casual? Is it excited or subdued, blunt or direct, or is it soothing, offering trust, security, and peace of mind?

Embed your brand voice in every communication you have with your clients. Use it in web content, marketing, and advertising. Display it in interviews, videos, speeches, and one-on-one encounters with your client.

The more consistent you are in the tone and language of your brand voice the stronger your brand will be. This is essential so you can attract and retain clients.

Once your brand tone is established, you need to focus on your brand language. Put together a clearly defined language guideline, using the tone, keywords, and phrases you already identified.

These guidelines form the communication standard for those people in your organization who have contact with your prospects and clients. It's important that you, and others who represent your brand, maintain this consistent experience for your client.

In my work as a mentalist, I focus on nonverbal communication. As a hypnotist, I focus more on linguistics.

To create an amazing and hypnotic client experience, we need to examine these two different areas of communication, verbal and body language. They are related to and affect the perception of your brand. Right now, we'll focus on verbal language.

Pronouns refer to people. Let's look at how you plan to refer to your client.

Let's use a medical professional for example who may take a more formal approach and say something like, "Patients at our facility are treated with the utmost care." It may sound too casual and nonspecific to say, "You'll get the best care possible."

Your word choice and economy of words is important to consider as you lay out your specific message guidelines.

For example, if you want to convey quick and direct language, you would eliminate extra wording and trim your sentences down. Instead of saying "be able to" you might say "can."

You might take complex sentences and cut them down into smaller bites. Here are some examples:

"Our establishment first opened its doors in 1982 after we initially exhibited our goods for the first time at a local fair."

"Our company opened in 1982, after exhibiting at a local fair."

You can clarify which words to use in place of others. For example, "but" versus "however" or "like" versus "such as."

As for verbs, you might set a guideline of using only active verbs and avoiding passive verbs. Your instructions to the people who represent your brand would be to speak in present tense as opposed to the future or past tense.

You can get as general or as detailed as you want. If it's just you with no support staff, still give this some thought and put effort into this.

There may be certain words you'd like to designate as taboo. These might be words that conjure up negative connotations, or words you feel may paint your brand in a bad light.

One of the biggest tone considerations is how formal or casual you want your presentation to be. This is a good time to consider your target audience. What do you know about them, such as, age range, or gender? What other characteristics do you know, which might include their likes and dislikes, and characteristics, such as familiarity or region. Then change your message and how you present your content accordingly.

My brand voice alters slightly based on the medium on which I'm communicating. For example, even as I just typed this last sentence, I was aware that I wouldn't speak this formally to my younger Instagram audience.

Here's how I would communicate this same message on Instagram: "Hey, when you're reaching out to your audience, remain true to who you are, while connecting on their level."

Same message. Both times, it's just me expressing naturally in a way which is relatable. Not contrived. Even as I type these words, there's no deep analytical thought involved. You, too, will find this comes naturally as you absorb and practice the guidelines you create.

If you choose a casual tone, create guidelines regarding the use of slang and swearing. For slang, pay close attention to your audience. A surfboard retailer would use different slang than a seller of comic books. The slang you choose should speak directly to your audience. It should be the slang they use. When using slang, you must still strive to be professional.

Be aware, slang goes out of style. As slang usage changes, you'll need to update your content. You'll also have to keep yourself up to date on which slang terms your audience uses.

Carefully written guidelines will ensure you avoid situations that could embarrass you.

Recently, while watching a Tony Robbins documentary, I was surprised with his use of words. Though I'm familiar with Tony Robbins, it has been some years since I had listened to or read his material. Over the past decade, I lost touch with his style. So, it shocked me when I heard him using the F word a lot. Like every second word it seemed. This doesn't seem to hurt his brand. He has made a choice and seems comfortable with it. To each their own.

I've seen this work for other brands as well, such as a restaurant which tries to emulate a New York style of service by being rude and swearing. That's part of the experience they are intentionally providing. It's certainly a distinct choice, and one which will influence people to choose or avoid your brand.

I err on the side of caution and avoid using foul language. Used in an inappropriate context, the use of such language could have damaging consequences for your brand image. My motto, which I adopted early on as a corporate speaker and entertainer is, "When in doubt, leave it out."

If you're dealing with many people who represent your brand to the public, I suggest you get as specific as possible. Designate the words that are okay to use and words that should be avoided. After all, this is your business, and you should protect it.

This is where understanding your brand voice, and the avatar of your client becomes important. Once you have that in place, making these decisions is simple and natural.

When faced with using jargon and technical terms, it's better to err on the side of simpler language. Your audience may not know a lot of technical words and you risk making them feel uninformed or stupid. If you get it wrong, it may make you look unprepared...or stupid.

For some niches, it's important to take the time to learn the jargon familiar to your audience. If you're doing something related to a hobby, music, computers, golf, or magic, then using a specialized vocabulary shows you go that extra mile to provide a familiar experience. This will reflect favorably on your brand voice.

However, there are niches where it may not be cool to use jargon. In the health or finance industries, for example. You risk either talking over your audience's head and alienating them or just sounding like you're reading from a textbook.

Humor is a huge part of my brand voice. It shows up in an obvious and overt way when I perform my comedy mind-reading and hypnosis shows. This doesn't show up the same way in this book. When I present this same material live as a speaker, I inject humor to connect and resonate with my audience. It wouldn't play out the same way in this written form.

I enjoy making people laugh on a day-to-day basis. If it's a big part of who you are, then consider implementing more humor and fun into your brand voice.

You'll need to examine whether humor is okay for your target market or not. If you're selling sensitive B2B products and working diligently at getting a message across, you'll want to maintain a more professional tone and use humor with caution.

If you're a dog trainer, it's great to use humor. This is also true for any industry where you're providing products and services to people passionate about something that brings joy to their life.

When used appropriately, humor can also help with acceptance of your message. For example, with medical and financial professionals who deal with serious matters regularly, humor can help your audience relax and be more receptive.

Humor is part of a more intimate form of communication and you need to understand your audience well and know what they consider funny. It's easy to miss the mark and come across in a way that's offensive or just not funny. Be careful here since this can create an uncomfortable and embarrassing situation.

The safest form of comedy is self-deprecating humor, where you make fun of yourself. You refer to qualities unique to you and make jokes about them. Admitting your quirks and making light of them is an excellent way to make yourself likable.

It can also cause people to think you're weird. For example, some of my friends refer to me as "bubble boy" because I'm cautious about germs and I dislike shaking hands. There are a few other weird things about me, but we don't really need to get into them right now!

Anyway, this often leads to humor at my expense which I'm okay with. I understand why many people would find this funny and even peculiar.

Anytime you venture into new markets pay close attention to regional differences. Consider this when researching your target market.

Typically, there are different cultural and environmental aspects you may need to understand. Of course, you know you're no longer selling products and services, rather you're sharing your brand experience. This makes it even more important for you to know about demographic and environmental differences.

It's as simple as if you're selling ice fishing gear to people in the far north, you might talk about how cold and snowy it is. On the other hand, if your target market is more likely to be sipping a mint julep on the porch during a sweltering summer afternoon, you'll want to take a different approach. You could use different language depending on whether your audience members are city dwellers or country folk.

Also, consider accents and idioms. If your audience is mostly American Southerners, for example, work a Southern accent into your brand tone in a subtle and authentic way.

Going back to talking about humor, I've entertained and provided marketing programs in the UK. It took a little while to understand and integrate English humor into my presentations.

As I developed this more, I found I could relate in a quicker and more effective way with my English audience. This occurred as more of their sense of humor became ingrained in my brand voice.

I'd like you to create your unique language guide or chart that documents the decisions you've made about what type of language you should use. Think of this as a formal guide and create it with clear instructions that anyone in your organizations can follow.

Read it over and make sure it's clear. Also have someone else read it, who understands you and your brand. See if they understand the message you're hoping to get across.

Write three adjectives to describe your brand voice tone. This is how you want your content to sound. It's the general feel or vibe of your brand.

For example, if your personality is humorous, then your tone would specify the type of humor you use. Is it sarcastic humor? Dry humor? Self-deprecating humor?

Think about the words you'll use in places like social media, website pages, marketing content, and in conversations with your clients.

How to Have Your Brand Voice Heard

Implement your brand voice to create a consistent experience for your clients wherever they have a connection with you.

The first step is to identify different marketing channels where the public will experience your brand.

As you know, consistency is of utmost importance. You need to think of every channel through which people may encounter you. I'll give you some ideas to get you brainstorming in this direction.

We're in the internet age. Your internet presence is of utmost importance and in many cases, is your primary media for communicating with the public. Your net presence includes such things as your website, your blog, various social media profiles, and any content you publish online. This includes content about you that isn't under your control. It all sends a message about your brand.

There are a lot of jokes and stories about how some sales presentations portray a product as something much more attractive than what you actually get.

In real life, it's not funny being disappointed during that post-purchase experience.

Perfect the smaller touch points such as your invoices and receipts, confirmations, thank you emails, follow-up emails, and replies to inquiries. Even these seemingly trivial matters communicate something about you and your brand to your client.

If this seems like too much effort, then have comfort in knowing your competitors feel the same way. They likely haven't even been exposed to this message. Many people reading this right now may agree it makes sense, but still won't make any changes. I hope that isn't you. Your return on investment to follow through and implement what I'm teaching you right now is astronomical.

Do you want better leads and bigger sales? Do you want to make more money, have more fun and help more people? Do you want to attract, keep, and grow customers?

Don't drop the ball in this area. You'll find ways to deliver and follow up consistent with the experience you promised. Many of your competitors won't do this. This is an area where you can differentiate your brand and make your completion vanish into thin air. It's like magic!

Video is one of the most powerful forms of communication these days. If you use video, it's important to pay attention to the words you use and the tone of your content. This includes what you post on various video sites, and videos created through webinars or media appearances. When appearing in a video be consistent with your brand voice.

Tom Hanks is a great example of someone who has established his brand as not only an amazing actor but a wonderful person. He's proven this time and time again as he encounters the public and displays genuine warmth and good nature. He participates in video pranks and pretty much goes along with whatever people want, within reason I'm sure.

Since we're talking about celebrities, there are others who have done the opposite. Their brands have been hurt or destroyed. For example, Michael Richards, a.k.a. Kramer from Seinfeld, was caught on video making racist statements. That ended his career.

There are many other examples of people who get away with their public display of prejudice, but that doesn't mean it's okay.

Anyway, back to us regular people. Your live interactions include those with your prospects, clients, interviews, presentations, your presence at a trade show, and chance encounters in an elevator. Staying on brand isn't always easy. But it's always important.

A lot of businesses have stopped using printed materials altogether. If you're still using print, consider things such as flyers, brochures, packaging, paperwork, letterhead, business cards. Make sure you remain on brand with the words you use in your tone and presentation to maintain a consistent brand experience which is expected by your clients.

How would you feel if you received a package which wasn't consistent with serving the environment from a company whose brand portrays it as socially conscious and environmentally friendly? This happened to me recently, and I won't be ordering from that company anymore. See, how the little things that are often overlooked can help you attract and retain clients, or lose them altogether.

Create guidelines for your employees or outsourced client service people regarding your brand voice when they communicate online or in person with clients. If you're a B2B company, for example, you probably want to present a more formal image that engenders trust. If you're a surfboard shop, you can allow your employees to say stuff like "hang loose" and "catch ya later, man."

Keep your tone consistent even when communicating with other businesses, whether they be suppliers or joint venture partners. You never know what sort of an attitude someone will have towards you if suddenly they see a different side of you. It's good practice to maintain your brand consistency at all times.

Storytelling can bring to life the voice and tone of your brand. Stories are great for conveying your values and creating a personal experience that engenders trust and develops a strong connection. For example, GoPro is all about creativity and innovation. They feature selected YouTube videos from clients that show how the client is using their products in creative ways.

In the next chapter of this book, as we create your message experience for your clients, we cover stories in great detail. You'll create and develop your story. It will be fun and interesting for you to dig into what's unique and special about you, your company, and your brand, and format that into stories which will help you deliver an amazing and hypnotic client experience. This is one of the most powerful things you can do for your business.

For now, though, I'll just touch on storytelling and lay some groundwork for you. That way when we get to the chapter on stories, the work you do now will move you along faster and help you be more productive.

There are a variety of story types for us to work with and for you to choose and develop.

With personal stories, you may want to share how you created your company or overcame a significant personal or business challenge.

You can get into stories of why and how you developed certain products or services and how it solved a problem for you, someone you know, or your first clients. Your story can be about how your clients have improved their lives or solved their problems using your products or services.

Maybe a behind-the-scenes story involving a specific employee or some of your employees would make sense and display the human face of your organization.

Another popular and powerful type of story is one that shows how you helped a specific client go from where they were to where they want to be. This can be done as a case study.

As you can see, storytelling can be used in many areas of your marketing in countless different ways. You can tell a story on your website or through social media. Your print materials can feature stories about employees or the founding of the company. Stories are useful for videos and effective as a way to spice up your promotional copy.

Your stories need to be captivating and relevant to your audience, much the same way stories are used in television commercials and shows, and movies. A story can be an anecdote in a speech or humor in a blog post.

The stories you pick and the words you use to tell it, should reinforce the voice and tone of your brand.

Once you've compiled all the information we've been working on in this chapter, remember to share it with everyone who has anything to do with communicating on behalf of your brand. Put together a document or manual, and distribute it. Make a habit of following up to ensure your guidelines are being followed.

Your guideline manual will include everything about your client persona, and the tone and language of your brand. Think of it as a comprehensive go-to reference manual when drafting content for external communications.

Your guidelines should be written in a PDF or other type of document easy to share. Divide it into sections that correspond to target client information with specific language guidelines, and any information on where the guidelines should be implemented.

Even if you're a solopreneur, perhaps an entertainer, coach, or speaker, and you handle everything yourself, you'll still need a guide. This makes everything so much easier when you face questions and decisions as you roll out any new advertising or marketing initiatives. By putting this together, you further ingrain these guidelines in your mindset. Believe me, the magic will unfold as these principles become ingrained in your brand and part of who you are and what you represent.

If you have other people representing your brand, then it's essential you create this manual. The information should be thorough and complex, so it's best to offer summaries to be used for quick reference.

When you or your people are writing content, or preparing to meet a client, this manual will be a lifesaver. It helps you save time and remain consistent when you need to check a certain point or answer a specific question quickly.

Like everything, with practice and repetition, your brand tone will become more natural as you use it. At some point, the guide may not even be needed or may become just a useful quick reference.

Be specific and give examples. Your team members need to see how your brand voice looks in print. They need to see the guidelines in action. This will give them a better idea of how they can use it themselves.

You may want your language guidelines to show examples of what NOT to do. Make sure this is clearly stated and explain why and how it can damage your brand.

If there are differences in how your brand tone is written for different channels, specify this with examples. For instance, like me, you may take a more casual tone in your social media or email newsletter, but maintain a more formal tone on your website or in your print materials.

Your guidelines should be written in your brand tone. This creates consistency and also shows your team members exactly how they are to write. It gives them a feel for it.

Creating all this material takes time and effort. Be patient and make sure it's done thoroughly. If you have team members, enlist them in creating your manuals. A fun and effective way to do that would be to do things like role-playing a variety of situations where they react and clarify what's outlined in your document.

Once you complete the guideline, give it to your team members. Also, share it with others involved with your brand voice, like any outsourced content creators or client service representatives. Offer a training session, during which you can go over each part of the guideline document and make sure everything is clear.

Allow for plenty of Q&A, and make sure everyone is on the same page.

Make this training and material a part of the onboarding of all new hires. You should also have your guidelines present when you train employees on client service or work on development and launches. It should be there at every step of the process.

Put someone in charge of ensuring the consistency and implementation of your brand voice. Create a process for reviewing the materials and making sure they are up to date. Many companies create a marketing checklist before any piece is published or goes into production. You could designate a Brand Voice Manager and ensure they sign off on all material.

Keep in mind this shouldn't be a one-time exercise. Your brand voice will change and evolve as your business goes through changes. There may be changes in the market to which you need to adapt. Regularly work with your team to review and modify your brand voice. It's good to do this on a quarterly basis at least. Look at real-life case studies and examples to see what is and isn't resonating with your audience.

Even if you're the only person on your team, work this out and review it regularly to make sure you're staying on track.

If you haven't already done so, list the areas of your business where you want your brand voice to be heard.

Highlight a story you can share. Make it one that tells something important about you, or your company. Or, share a story featuring a big win for one of your clients. Choose a story that reflects your brand's voice.

Outline the key people responsible for implementing your brand's voice and determine who will monitor this, so the process is completed.

CHAPTER FOUR: YOUR STORY

When I was five years old, I met my uncle, a Las Vegas magician. He taught me my first magic trick. That was the moment I became fascinated by the art and science of performing magic.

I did my first show at the age of ten. While in high school, I earned a five-figure annual income performing shows on weekends. When I graduated high school, I turned professional.

Performing magic shows didn't seem like work. In fact, there was nothing I loved doing more. I was blessed to find something I enjoyed that also provided income for me at a young age.

One thing I learned early on was the importance of the business part of show business. Performing was only part of it. Running my business was also important.

I took it upon myself to learn and innovate in the area of business and marketing. I also enjoyed the business side of show business.

As a result, during the last three decades, I've done several thousand shows. Many of these are repeat bookings because I make a point of over-delivering both on and off the stage.

Much of what I share as an educator in speeches, seminars, courses and books like this, is based on my experience marketing myself as a corporate speaker and entertainer. Oh, and, by the way, I just used the power of storytelling to explain how I got started in marketing. Simple and effective.

Aha, by sharing this personal story, which I hope was interesting to you, it's much more likely you'll remember some key points. And, sharing personal stories brings us closer together. You know a little more about me, and how my experience can benefit what you're working to accomplish.

I could continue with this story and share more examples and many learning lessons. In fact, I will share more throughout this book. Real life stories can teach, bond, and persuade.

Many studies show likability is a primary driver of consumer choice. There are plenty of ways to make yourself more likable. A good story about yourself or your brand is the most powerful and memorable way for you to do that. Personal stories are an effective way to build rapport.

Likability created by a good story has more impact and a greater influence on a client than any other factor. In fact, studies prove, it does this by a factor of three to one for television commercials and two to one for print ads. Meaning, the same ad with a story versus one without a story theme is far more effective in persuading and generating business.

A good example is Subaru's *They Lived* commercial. It opens with images of hunks of a scrapped car on the road. Seeing this footage, the viewer assumes that the passengers perished in the crash. But each image ends by saying, "They lived." The emotions and the suspense created by the video lead the viewer to form a psychological connection with Subaru.

The brain is stimulated and is engaged in specific ways when it hears a story. A story relates to people. It activates areas related to sensory stimuli such as the temporal cortex, which is associated with language. While I'm not a doctor, I like to study this stuff. It's fascinating and relates directly to my work as a public speaker and magical entertainer.

Words and actions trigger the same areas in the brain. The brain doesn't distinguish between something that's real or imagined.

Compare this to what the brain does when it takes in facts and data. When looking at data, the language areas of the brain light up, but not the emotional and sensory areas. Stories trigger these. This means your story engages your audience in ways data cannot. Besides thinking, your audience feels and experiences the story.

Do you remember how old I was when I started as a magician?

Chances are if I didn't weave that data into a story, you would've forgotten by now.

It's possible you don't remember, however, it's more likely you do. You may recall, I was five years old when my uncle first showed me magic tricks.

The story was about how I started in marketing as a necessity to be successful in show business. That will likely stick with you because of the way I presented the information. And that was the primary message my story intended to get across. The message also included a benefit to you, my reader.

People forget statistics and facts. They are less likely to forget a good story.

This is especially true if your story conveys a message your audience cares about deeply. When a story is told along with compelling data, people are more emotionally and intellectually engaged.

Stories are memorable. Not only because of the emotional connection but also, they stand out. Amid all the content clutter on the internet, a story gets attention.

Think for a moment of the many articles you can find online that offer tips for doing something. For example, *Five Tips for Writing a Memorable Blog*. You've seen articles like these. They are all generic. But what if you found a compelling story that shares those same tips? That's something you'd be more likely to pay attention to and remember.

Stories are more important in marketing and business now more than ever. The explosive growth of social media and content marketing has created a cluttered mess. You need to stand out to get attention. For you to stand out from the crowd, you have to inform and entertain.

When you provide an experience which educates and entertains, you'll be more memorable. Your audience will associate you, your story, and your brand with the product or service you provide.

There's no better way to be remembered than with great stories.

Stories create an emotional connection between your target market and your product or brand. Stories have a psychological effect. This adds tremendous power to your marketing and propels the growth of your brand.

Don't limit yourself. Good storytelling isn't just for people who are natural storytellers. You can be a good storyteller. There are tricks and processes to make this easy for anyone. I'll share insights with you to help you with storytelling.

In this chapter, we'll take the time to understand why storytelling needs to be a big part of your content marketing. Storytelling is important, regardless of what product or service you provide.

We'll identify different types of stories and how they are used. We'll examine company and brand stories, personal stories, client stories, and bedtime stories. Just kidding, I threw bedtime stories in there just to see if you're paying attention. Are you?

We'll look at the stories that have stood the test of time. We'll assess which ones have the greatest impact and then look at how you can use these in your client centric marketing.

We'll identify which stories connect best with your specific target market. By the time you've finished this chapter, you'll put stories together and tie them into your marketing and content creation.

We'll go over the key elements that will make your story effective, regardless of the story format you use. We'll look at the different media such as videos and articles, and draft your plan for finishing and producing your story.

Now, I want you to think about some of your favorite brand stories. What stories do you remember easily? What stories come to mind?

What makes those stories memorable to you?

The Best Stories to Share

Before we look at story formats and story elements, we need to discuss the kinds of stories to tell.

The story of your company or brand is a go-to type story. These are important; they support how and why you created your brand image.

Your company story will include how your company came into existence and how it grew to its current state. Often told by the founder, your story will convey the values and culture of your organization. Sometimes, if the company is large, the story might be told by some of the first employees.

There will be opportunities for you to include other formats. Examples are rags to riches, overcoming challenges, case studies, and other time-tested formulas.

A good example of a brand story is one of Nike's waffle-tread shoes. The story tells us that Nike co-founder, Bill Bowerman, one day in a fit of inspiration, poured rubber into a waffle iron, giving birth to the waffle-tread. This story tells you the company is innovative and not afraid to try out crazy ideas that could revolutionize shoes.

If you're like me, and function primarily as a solopreneur, your personal story is most likely going to make sense as your foundational story.

The story can be how you overcame difficulties or challenges. The story can relate how you moved past a challenge and achieved success. The story describes where you were and where you are now.

For example, you might write a story about a time when you couldn't manage your time well. You were always busy and had way too many things to do and no free time to do what you enjoyed. This is the setting of the story. Your story might then go to relate how you discovered a simple and handy technique for managing time better, which helped you get more done and have more time to yourself.

You can tell stories that relate to products. Tell a story about how your product was developed. Or, describe what problem it solves. Your story can explain challenges faced when developing the product. A client-focused story can show how a client uses your product in a creative way.

One way to discover great product stories is to ask your clients to write the stories for you. This is a fine use of crowdsourcing. You turn part of your content creation over to your audience. Crowdsourcing is an effective content marketing strategy because it gets your audience actively engaged. Your story becomes their story. Their story becomes your story. This gives your clients buy-in with your success.

A client story is one in which your client relates somehow to your product or service. This is one of the best types of stories because it emphasizes the benefits of what you offer.

When people read about a client's experience with your brand, they can put themselves in the client's place. This helps them understand how your products or services can benefit them. These stories are also great because they are authentic. It's always better to have someone else tell people how great you are, rather than you telling others how great you are.

A client story can focus on a common problem your market faces and how one particular client overcame this problem with your product. For example, if you sell financial planning services, you could ask clients to send their stories about how they struggled on their own or with not so effective planners in the past.

The story can relate how things changed when they connected with you and everything became clear and simple. The story finishes by stating how their expectations regarding returns on investment have been exceeded.

Employee stories are engaging because they take people behind the scenes and add a human element to your company. Your audience gets a glimpse of the inner workings of your company and how every person involved makes a difference. These stories also help to convey your corporate culture.

An employee story might feature a particular employee and how they improved a product or service. Or, perhaps how they helped the company reach important goals, or helped a client in need. Another employee story might be their history of how and why they came to the company. An employee story is something personal or professional about someone who works for your company. Effective stories must resonate with your audience.

A case study is a more detailed and researched story of a person, group, activity, event, or problem. The case study concept comes from the social sciences. However, companies form them for exploring business problems and challenges. Case studies also include recommended solutions. One form, the historical case study, can be used the same way you use your company story.

The main difference between a case study and other story types we discussed is the level of thoroughness. A case study includes a great deal of research and organization. A case study might look like a detailed retelling of your company's history or the development of a product.

Case studies are an effective way to convey the benefits of doing business with you. Especially when you present the case study in a manner relatable to your target audience.

Okay, so what's your story?

Consider the different stories I shared with you. Which one would be easiest and fastest for you to create right now?

What content do you already have?

Make some notes on these ideas as you'll need them later on as we complete this chapter.

The 7 Best Story Formats

Once you have some story ideas, you need to decide which mediums you'll use. There are different types of media outlets from which to choose. Knowing your target audience will help you make the best choices.

Look at the data you have on your target market. Notice how we keep coming back to looking at data on your target market? What kind of media do they consume?

Some people like reading text content while others don't. Certain psychographics and demographics prefer images or videos. You'll need to look at the content your market already consumes to make these decisions.

If you don't already have the data or want to double check your data, here are several ways you can do it.

Website and social media analytics give you objective data on your audience's online activities. You can see which pages they visit and on which pages they spend the bulk of their time.

See what kind of content your target market shares on social media. Click on the links they share and see what content is most popular. You may see a pattern. For example, you might discover your audience shares videos instead of articles. Or your audience shares statistics and not poetry. These patterns will depend on who they are and what they do.

Look at blogs and websites in niches that are similar to yours. These are blogs or websites that share the same audience as you. See what kind of content these sites post and, more importantly, the audience's reaction to it. Look for content that has a lot of comments and activity.

As I've said many times before, simply the best way to get information is to ask your clients. Ask them what kind of media they like. You can ask them on your social media pages, your blog, or any other online marketing channel.

If you don't have an available client base to ask, just run a small and inexpensive online campaign to get the data you need. Create a survey to collect data. Be transparent by letting them know you're striving to provide the type of content they want in the way they want to receive it.

In addition to telling stories in person, which you would do as a speaker, coach, or in a sales presentation, you can tell a story using any type of media at all, from single images to long-form videos.

Many stories are told in text. To write your story in text takes planning. You should outline your story and make sure all the key elements are included.

When writing the story, don't try to sound lofty and academic. Appeal to an average person. Write using a simple, personal tone your audience can relate to and understand. If you're not a seasoned writer yourself, don't worry about it as long as it's genuine and sincere. You'll get your point across and create impact.

Video is one of the best ways for you to tell a story. A video doesn't have to be long or complex. Production doesn't have to be high end. The key is to tell your story, even if it's as simple as sharing a case study or client testimonial.

Images tell stories by suggesting to the viewer what's going on or what happened to produce the image. An image can be an illustration, a photograph, or a series of images. Infographics can be powerful and effective.

Many of the most famous photographs leave a lasting impression because of the stories they tell. Just think of images of the aftermath of a disaster, like the giant tsunami that struck Japan in 2011, or the photo of the sailor kissing his bride after returning from the war.

These photos capture a moment in a story, and the viewer's mind fills in the rest. There was a memorable photo of a couple kissing during the hockey riots in Vancouver where I live. It's forever etched in my mind. And not our city's proudest moment.

Animation offers an alternative to videos and photos. A creative video can be entertaining and effective. Animation software programs can be easier than producing video footage.

An advantage of cartoon animations is they make it simple to create branded content. You can use the same characters, design, themes, or structure, so your cartoons are consistent. This consistency helps communicate your brand.

In other words, when someone sees your cartoon, they know unmistakably it's your brand.

An infographic is a visual representation of data or other information. The point of an infographic is to make statistical data, which is pretty dry to read as text, interesting and easier to understand.

Earlier, I mentioned you should avoid facts and figures in your stories. Infographics offer a great way to share facts and figures in a way that's like a story.

Think in terms of character, plot, and other story elements. You can create an infographic that conveys its data in an entertaining and engaging way.

You can tell a story or use stories in your live events such as webinars and offline events. In fact, a story provides a good basis for an event.

If you're going to host a webinar on how to build a website, you can create a character that's a frustrated small business owner, hopeless at doing anything internet related. Use the story of this business owner as the plot of your webinar. This will make it more interesting and relatable to your audience.

When considering the type of media to use for storytelling, don't let a lack of resources, tools, or skill stop you from using the perfect medium.

Video, for example, seems to present challenges to those who've never worked with video before. There are tools and resources available to make content creation easy, no matter what your skill level.

I'm not naturally tech savvy or good with video editing, but I do some of it myself. At the very least, I take the time and make an effort to get to a point where I could do it myself. Though ultimately, I'll outsource this type of work.

Look around and figure out what type of content your market consumes and shares the most. Make notes of what you find and fill in any blanks from earlier work you've done.

Identify and decide which media you're going to use. You can start by choosing one from the suggestions I've made in this chapter, or you can look at the media used by different companies and brands you admire.

Once you've written and produced your story in at least one format, you'll have to decide exactly where to distribute it. There are many outlets you can use, and we have already discussed some of the channels. The goal is to choose a distribution channel that will get your story in front of as many people as possible in your target market.

Just as you did when choosing which media to use, look at your audience to figure out which distribution channel to focus on first. Find out where and how they consume content online using the methods we discussed earlier.

An easy venue for your stories is your website and blog. Many companies include their company story as part of their website's About page. In fact, for good branding, every aspect of your site should help convey your brand story to your visitors.

Personal stories and client stories make great blog content. Blogging has always been about telling personal stories. That's what the medium was created for. A blog is a weblog or an online journal. The key to blogging personal stories well is to add takeaways to your stories. These are tips or insights drawn from the story that can help the reader directly.

Any content distribution strategy will likely include social media. Social media use is massive among all demographics. It's growing every year and will continue to be where people hang out online. People use social media to enjoy and share content. They want to be entertained and engaged, so this is a perfect venue for sharing your stories.

Each social media website has its set of demographics or content sharing limitations. You should know which sites your audience use as well as the general demographic for each social media channel you use.

Learn the limitations of the channels you choose to use. You can share any type of content on most social media sites. Other sites impose a character limit, which means you either have to tell a compelling story in a small amount of characters or provide a link to that story. Some sites are made for video sharing and also considered to be social media channels.

There are some sites that are directories for certain types of content. For example, there are article directories or websites for sharing images. These are good places to get your stories out to people who don't already know about your brand or aren't already connected to you.

If you're doing email marketing, your goal is to get as many emails you send out opened by the recipient. Make storytelling an integral part of the emails you send your subscribers. This will boost your open rates and also help to spread your brand image. Any time you create and distribute a story on another channel, be sure to let your email list know about it too.

If you have a budget for paid ads, this is a great place to use your stories. A story is much more powerful than a promotional advertisement, so it's a good way to get the most for your advertising dollar.

Look at every communication channel where you're in touch with your audience. See if there's a way you can add your stories there. If you participate in online forums, use a story to introduce a thread or topic. If you're doing an offline direct mail campaign, create a great story to use as an introduction.

Vary your media types and distribution channels. At first, it's best to choose one and get it going before adding the next. Simply spraying your stories all over the web takes great effort and produces minimal results. It's better to identify the media type and channel you feel is the best and start there.

One of the reasons it's important to start small is you need to track your results carefully. Set goals for views, shares, purchases, or other metrics that define success for you. You can then monitor the results of your efforts and see clearly which is working and which isn't. With this data, you know which distribution channels to drop because they're not performing. You'll also know which channels to focus more of your efforts on because they produce results.

Tracking all this can be tedious. It's extra work, and most marketers don't do it. It's worth the effort though, and you'll be amazed what you learn when you start tracking the information. This effort will pay off as you use your data to improve your return on investment.

Your marketing will be so much better when you have data. It allows you to outshine your competition and at a cost lower than what your competition pays. Most likely, they don't take the time to know their metrics.

Although each story may focus on an individual channel, it's good to modify your stories so you can tell them on other channels as well. For example, if you're producing videos, you can take still images from your video at key moments and release them on social media. When you modify and use your stories on other channels, you get the most mileage out of them and can also reach another audience.

Always encourage your audience to share your stories. If you're lucky, one just might go viral and bring a great deal of business your way. Make it easy to share your stories with buttons and add-ons for social media sharing. Come right out and ask your audience to share if they like something you publish.

Review your analytics or other information you have about your online presence. If you don't have any information yet, look at the channels I've mentioned in this chapter. Notice where your audience spends the most time.

Make sure your story is easy to share when you post it. Decide on the call-to-action and buttons you'll use on each channel that includes a sharing option.

Modify your story to work best on each channel.

Once you start creating and posting stories, it's important to monitor feedback from your audience. Few people can get it right the first time. Through feedback from your audience, you'll constantly refine your stories until they have the desired impact. Big brands have been telling their stories for a long time, and this is why they do it so well.

You now know why stories are important. You know how stories work to build an emotional connection with your audience. You have ideas on what types of stories you can tell.

You know the elements of a good story and the basics of creating an engaging plot.

You also know how to make your stories as effective as possible by creating an emotional connection. You know how to create a plan for producing and distributing your stories.

So, which distribution channels will you focus on first for distributing your story?

7 Powerful Story Plots

Since the dawn of human existence, stories have been a major part of our lives. As soon as early humans developed the ability to speak and think symbolically, stories were told.

The only difference between the stories told today and those from ancient times is the setting and the content. The storylines have remained the same, from the first human stories from ten thousand years ago to the stories we watch today on television or at the movies.

The reason these storylines are so enduring, is they speak to fundamental emotions we all understand and experience.

The themes relate to what we all face as human beings. These classic plots in our story planning help us create something effective and emotional for our audience.

There's no need to reinvent the wheel. Let's go over seven widely published, and timeless formats you can use.

Different people have given different names to these seven basic plots, but they all boil down to much the same thing.

The seven basic story plots are:

1. Conquering the Monster

2. Rags to Riches

3. The Quest

4. Voyage and Return

5. Tragedy

6. Comedy

7. Rebirth

Now, let's have a look at each one and some examples to help you get started.

Conquering the Monster is a familiar story line. You'll recognize this if you've ever seen a horror or science fiction movie. We can find this in one of the first known works of literature, the *Epic of Gilgamesh*, from the ancient Sumerian civilization.

The hero, Gilgamesh, goes on a quest during which he battles monsters. The storyline is also the format used in many video games like Super Mario Brothers. If you're somewhere around my age, you may remember that game. Or, if you're just a bit older than I, perhaps you played it and just don't remember!

In a Conquering the Monster story, the hero goes on a journey that culminates in the defeat of a terrible monster. The odds are stacked against the lowly hero. Through strength, cunning, and other virtues, the hero overcomes the monster.

You've seen this storyline in the biblical story of David and Goliath. It's the plot of many classics of literature such as Beowulf. It's the basic plot behind *Godzilla*, *The Terminator*, *Star Wars*, and the James Bond movies. It's also one of the main themes in superhero comic books.

The key is that the monster doesn't have to be an actual monster. It can be any problem or frustration your audience faces.

One great example in marketing is the Allstate Mayhem campaign. The character Mayhem is a metaphor for any disaster you could face, and you conquer this monster through insurance.

Another good example is Nike's Just Do It narrative, where athletes overcome the monster, whether it be fear of failure or lack of confidence.

The next story type is **Rags to Riches**. The classic American dream story is an example of a rags-to-riches story. Imagine the story of a poor immigrant, washed up on the shores of

America, only to pull themselves up by the bootstraps through their cunning and hard work. One day, they become the billionaire on the hill.

You can see this story in the lives of many early twentieth-century entrepreneurs like Nelson Rockefeller, or in authors such as J. K. Rowling. It appears in classic stories like *Cinderella* or Charles Dickens' *David Copperfield*. Films like *Rocky* and *Aladdin* portray rags-to-riches stories, and it's the storyline behind many of today's reality TV shows.

Rags-to-Riches stories can be used effectively to tell brand stories since most companies start out as shoe-string operations in someone's basement. A good example is the story of the app WhatsApp, which was developed by Ukrainian-born Jan Koum while he was on food stamps. He sold his company five years later to Mark Zuckerberg for $19 billion.

The Quest is another story type. With the Quest, the main character and their entourage set out on a mission to discover some place, person, or object. They face obstacles and hardships along the way, all of which they triumph over and then proceed on. This is an excellent storyline because it's exciting and keeps people on the edge of their seats, waiting for the next obstacle. The audience travels along with the heroes, vicariously experiencing trials, challenges, and discovery along with the hero.

The Arthurian legend of Sir Galahad's *Quest for the Holy Grail* is a classic example of the Quest. More modern examples include the *Indiana Jones* series, *The Lord of the Rings*, the *Harry Potter* series, the movie *Finding Nemo*, and one of the most famous quest stories, *The Wizard of Oz*.

The Quest storyline could be used in your search to discover or create a product that solves the problems and hardships that your audience faces.

From Homer (the poet, not Bart's dad) to Luke Skywalker, human cultures abound with stories about a hero's journey into a strange or dangerous world and finally return home.

The Quest story can be understood by anyone who has ventured away from home geographically or ventured outside their comfort zone psychologically. It strikes a chord with people. The eventual homecoming offers an emotional release. These stories are popular with children, maybe because the whole world to them is a strange land full of obstacles.

Some classics fit this mold like Homer's *Odyssey* and Lewis Carrol's *Alice in Wonderland*. Some fantasy and science fiction stories use this storyline.

Modern **Voyage and Return** stories include *Back to the Future* and the TV miniseries *Lost*, which I couldn't quite finish watching.

Voyage and Return stories can be used in a variety of different contexts. For example, you may have made a discovery while traveling that inspired you to come home and develop a product. Product development can be a voyage and return story if it involves venturing outside of your comfort zone. This story can also be used to sell travel-related products.

Tragedy stories are the toughest to use in marketing. They're based on some fatal character flaw, weakness, or lapse in morals by the main character, which gradually destroys them. Tragedies, like Shakespeare's *Macbeth*, feature an anti-hero who is haunted and tormented by their fatal flaw throughout the story, and they nearly always succumb to it in the end. For a tragedy, death is the happy ending. Examples of tragedies include *Bonnie and Clyde*, John Steinbeck's *Of Mice and Men*, *Westside Story*, and the movie *Titanic*. While it's good to be aware of this story type, generally tragedies aren't featured in marketing campaigns.

Comedy is the next story type we'll examine. Although comedies are funny, not every funny story is a comedy. The term comedy is used here in the Shakespearean sense. In a comedy, the plot involves confusion among the characters. This leads to a wide variety of shenanigans. Eventually, the confusion gets resolved. By the way, in acting school at year end, we presented *A Midsummer Night's Dream*. Big surprise, I was cast as the donkey character, named Bottom!

Most sitcoms use the confusion storyline for their episodes. This is because one mix-up offers an interesting plot and many opportunities for humor. Just take a look at any of your favorite comedies, whether a TV show or a movie.

Businesses can use the comedy format to reframe a problem into comedic confusion. A business, for example, may have an IT mix-up to untangle. In addition to following this storyline, you can add comedic elements to any story to make it more fun for the audience. Humor is a great emotion to trigger, and it makes your story more fun and memorable.

The **Rebirth** story is the last story type for us to consider. It can be used effectively in marketing. This is a story in which someone sinks to their lowest, most hopeless point, then makes a miraculous recovery. The struggle of the main character offers a conflict to the story. Struggling against great obstacles and rising from the ashes is inspirational and relatable to the audience.

In *A Christmas Carol*, Scrooge threatens to stop Christmas, but the three ghosts help Scrooge see the errors of his ways, and the holiday is saved. There's an element of rebirth in nearly every episode of *Doctor Who* or a James Bond movie. In these stories, the hero faces death but in the end, narrowly escapes. *Beauty and the Beast* and *Sleeping Beauty* are also rebirth stories.

Recently, Georganne at my dental office and I were sharing how we enjoyed the latest movie release of *Beauty and the Beast*. My ego was temporarily inflated when she said I could've played Gaston. My thoughts went to the image of this strong and handsome man. Then, I began to think about his severely flawed character. Perhaps, she was hinting as to my true nature!

There are many rebirth story ideas in a business context. Your product could save people right at the moment when they are at the very bottom. This plot can also be worked into a client testimonial.

Your brand story could be about your business facing hardship and near bankruptcy when your persistence and a great idea saves the day. Any personal story about overcoming a hardship or dark time is a rebirth story.

The Rebirth story you tell doesn't even have to be about your company, but can focus just on your clients instead. A great example is Gatorade's *Replay* series, which told the story of two ice hockey teams who took to the ice eleven years after a game which had involved a near fatal accident for one player.

The story isn't about Gatorade at all. Instead, Gatorade sponsors the game, and you only see their products peripherally in the footage. This video is worth searching and viewing online.

Keep in mind, an individual story can have several of these storylines within it. A hero may go on a journey to conquer a monster, only to face a serious and near-fatal struggle from which he/she experiences a rebirth, then returns home at the end. You don't have to restrict yourself to one storyline. Most great stories combine elements of a few.

Of the different classic story formats, which would resonate most with your brand? Start jotting down some ideas for what would go into your story

By now, you probably have some ideas swarming in your head about stories you can use for your brand, company, products, employees, or clients. The next step is to choose the story type that's most appropriate for your audience.

How to Choose Your Best Story Type

When it comes to storytelling, it's not the story itself that determines its effectiveness. Stories need to resonate with and affect your audience. For this to happen, you need to use the right types of stories.

Remember the work we did about getting to know your audience? When telling stories, we need to understand the values and emotions that will resonate most with your audience.

This is where, again, it's valuable for you to understand your target market's psychographic and demographic makeup. Knowing the age, economic situation, physical location, and gender, as well as psychographics including the thoughts, feelings, opinions, values, and attitudes of your market helps you connect on a deeper level.

The attitudes and values of our clients play a big part in storytelling. When your story is in sync with the attitudes and values of your audience, it will resonate with them in a powerful manner.

A good way to understand this is to look at two ad campaigns that speak to different values. Coca-Cola's *Build* video pans through the cross-section of a building to show the people who live in the building enjoying their day and, of course, drinking Coke. The families and couples range in diversity and age, from young couples with a baby to retirees.

However, conspicuously absent are any LGBT couples or other non-traditional families. We can assume this is because Coca-Cola considers its target audience traditional. A great deal of its client base is probably politically conservative.

On the other hand, Honey Maid's *This Is Wholesome* documentary series includes a family called *Dad and Papa* about a same-sex couple. Showing a same-sex family and saying, "This is wholesome" obviously appeals to a younger, more educated, and more progressive audience.

We can only assume when Coke's marketing experts determine its market's values have changed, Coke will change its marketing strategies.

To create effective stories, you must have a deep understanding of your audience. You must even go beyond psychographics and demographics. A good way to gain this information is to survey your clients.

Ask questions such as:

- Why did they buy from you?

- Why were they looking for a product like yours?

- What questions did they ask along the way?

Next, you need to identify the key emotions associated with your brand. These are the emotions your clients relate to when they consume your content, use your services, buy your products, and otherwise interact with your brand. These vary from brand to brand, and also from industry to industry and niche to niche.

For example, a family restaurant will appeal to different emotions in its stories than a law firm or a security software company. The law firm or security software company may appeal to fear or caution. A security company's story may involve a hero (you) conquering a monster (a hacking attack) using a special weapon (its software). A family restaurant may tell the story of a group of heroes (your family) conquering a different monster (the stress of daily life) by taking the kids out to enjoy good food and a good time.

Fundraising organizations often use compassion in their stories. This is what's happening when a starving child gazes out at you from your television. The target client is someone who is moved by compassion to donate. This is the emotion the stories of an organization such as this strive to elicit.

Even though your stories need to trigger emotions, they also need to be based on interesting topics. In fact, a good way to get ideas for stories is to ask your clients what interests they have.

Following the news and looking for stories or current events that may be of interest to your target market is a good way for you to find inspiration for your stories.

Another good source is content you previously published. See which of your videos have received the most views and which of your online posts have received the most likes and comments.

You can also look at your competitor's content and see what's popular with their audience, which could soon become your audience.

Follow your audience in forums, in social media, and anywhere else they interact online. Become a fly on the wall and listen to them. You can learn what interests them and use this information when developing your stories.

Authentic and relatable stories are the best way for you to communicate a message to your listeners. You can always find great stories by just looking around and keeping your eyes and ears open.

Get in the habit of telling stories about real events, real people, and real situations. Base your stories on topics you find interesting. Elaborate and tell a story that will inform and entertain your audience.

Of course, you're not going to tell stories for the sake of telling stories. There will always be a message supporting your brand, products, and services. Granted, this is usually done in an indirect way through your stories.

You know I'm a big fan of going to your clients for content. This holds true for your stories. You can get your clients to create stories for you.

Client-generated content is always best because it's authentic. It comes easily and quickly since you don't need to create anything from scratch. All you need to do is structure the content and elaborate on it.

You should listen to your clients on a regular basis. With stories in mind, just listen more intently and with greater interest. As you do this, you'll identify stories which you may have brushed off as an idle conversation in the past.

You can also become proactive and reach out to your clients. Ask them to create stories and send them to you. You'll be surprised at how many people take you up on this. And, from my experience, the quality of the stories from clients is quite good.

Which story is most effective for your market?

At this point, you should have a large bank of story ideas, so just pick one and get started.

How to Create Your Powerful Story

Engaging stories are a key to effective communication. Stories resonate with the listeners through an emotional connection.

Compassion gets donors to give money. Concern inspires consumers to buy and install security software on their computer. A sense of mystery and discovery drives stories of a quest. Fear and loathing of the terrible monster add suspense and excitement to conquering the monster stories.

Your story must be genuine and from the heart. It should connect with your audience's pain points, values, and desires.

Your story won't impact your audience unless they can relate to the characters in your story. Think back to any show you watched or book you read or listened to, only to find you didn't care what happened to the characters. Why was it boring? Perhaps because the story failed to engage you.

To stay engaged, we need to relate to the characters in the story. We want to cheer for the hero and hope they'll return home to conquer the monster and bounce back from a huge setback.

Compelling characters in your stories should reflect the values of your market. Choose characters your audience can identify with, the people who will make them say, "That man or woman is just like me." Or they might say, "I know someone like that." Use real people and real situations in your stories.

You'll find this easy to do once you get started. And it may even be fun for you.

Suspense and anxiety are important elements in any story. This is one way to keep audiences glued to the story to see what happens. We know James Bond won't get killed by the villain an hour into the movie, yet we're still on the edge of our seats as we watch the drill get closer to his head. Suspense and anxiety are more powerful in storytelling than the rational mind, which says, "That wouldn't happen."

Many stories, especially business and motivational ones, are inspirational. For telling stories in a marketing context, the goal is to inspire your audience to take action. You want them to make a decision to do business with you.

A fundraising commercial showing starving children isn't designed to drive you to despair and give up hope. It should inspire you, to let you know you can take action and make a difference.

Inspiration is important in a marketing context. It can influence a person to take action. Taking action can mean a product gets purchased, or a service gets used. At a subtle level, it may mean your brand and your vision gets recognized and supported.

A well-structured story has a clear beginning, middle, and end. The classic story is based on conflict and ultimate resolution. The conflict keeps us tuned in and engaged. It provides suspense and anxiety. Even though we know it will turn out well for our characters, the resolution at the end gives us a sense of release. This triggers positive emotions.

A great example of using structure to evoke emotion is the film *The Goonies*. A group of kids goes off in search of One-Eyed Willie's hidden treasure to save their home from foreclosure. The whole time, they're pursued by scary, yet buffoonish gangsters. There's suspense as the gangsters chase the kids. We feel anxious when the kids have trouble finding the treasure, and they come close to giving up. The story is resolved when they finally find the treasure, the gangsters are arrested, and the family avoids foreclosure.

In all good marketing stories, the product is in the background. Focus on telling good stories, and not on promoting the brand or product. Just like other forms of content marketing, your story will do the selling for you.

If you're telling a product story, the product will take center stage. Its benefits could be a major part of the story; however, less promoting is better.

The best stories reflect the benefits of the product without calling out the product by name. In the Subaru *They Lived* video, the story doesn't come right out and focus on the car brand. The story doesn't blatantly say, "Because they drove a Subaru and it has these outstanding safety features, they lived." The viewer makes that connection in their mind, and the connection is much stronger when it's made this way.

Another good story element is to make the story you're telling part of a much bigger story. It helps to advance the concept or idea behind the brand or product.

If you think back to Nike's Waffle Iron story, the audience learns how one of the founders created the waffle pattern. But what the story says is, "Nike is a company that innovates and changes the world."

In the stories you tell, let your brand personality play a major part. Red Bull tells stories of exceptional athletes since its brand personality is about extreme sports. Let your brand personality shine through.

One effective storytelling technique is to break up the story. Instead of telling the entire story all at once, offer just one scene or part of it. This is a good way to keep your audience tuned in for the next installment.

This is where you end your talk or advertisement with, "To be continued..."

Another idea you can play with is creating a story within a story. *The Arabian Nights* is an example of this. A more current example from Netflix is the anthology called *Black Mirror*. Each story in the collection of an anthology is an individual story that follows a similar theme or topic of the whole.

This is another way to keep your audience interested and engaged. They want to hear more of your stories since one story sets up interest in future stories. They're interested in the overall theme which relates back to your brand image.

Everyone wants to have their story or video go viral. The ones that go viral have one thing in common—they evoke strong emotions. These stories are awe-inspiring, moving, illuminating, amusing, amazing, shocking, scary, infuriating, or controversial. Or, they involve cats!

Spice up your stories with these emotions. Doing so will help get your stories heard, remembered, and shared. This will help your message get acted upon—as long as they're appropriate and relevant for your brand and audience.

Most people are visual. We relate more to images than to words or sounds. This is the reason we have an expression that says, "A picture is worth a thousand words." Adding visual elements to your story will make the story more memorable. Visual elements will also increase the likelihood your story will be shared.

You can create images to tell stories without using words or text. When advertising online, this allows you to get a message across in the flash of an image. Visual elements make stories more effective because they are excellent at triggering emotions.

Outline your story. If you're feeling creative, outline several stories. Use a variety of the techniques you've learned in this chapter.

PART THREE: MARKETING

"Marketing is built upon influence and persuasion."

CHAPTER FIVE: INFLUENCE MARKETING

After establishing credibility and expertise, you'll influence others. Your opinions and recommendations will matter. Your credibility and expertise allow you to be an influencer.

Your audience will share your thoughts, ideas, and the content you create. They'll take it to heart. People will respect your experience and trust your knowledge when they see you as an expert and acknowledge your credibility.

It's common for celebrities, authors, politicians, and industry leaders to have people hanging onto their every word. Their audience will recognize the value in what the influencer has to share. These followers are conditioned to believe they'll be rewarded by following his or her advice.

This ability to use your reputation to affect people's behavior is the power of influence. Leaders, who are consistent and care for their followers, can create great change based on their suggestions and recommendations.

When you market from a place of influence, you'll find it easy to grow your business. You'll do so in an ethical and productive way. As you build this goodwill among your client base, your word-of-mouth marketing will take on a life of its own. The retention rate of your clients and their lifetime value to your business will go through the roof.

This is truer today than it has been in the past. The balance of power between client and companies has changed. It will continue to change during this new economy we're all in right now.

People become wary and suspicious when they sense a sales pitch is being delivered. Online marketing is prevalent every minute of the day. This results in an overabundance of advertising messages. We deal with this by blocking out most of these efforts to gain our attention.

The people who are most sensitive to this are also the ones who can become your greatest clients. The people who are most turned off by direct marketing are also most easily persuaded by other means. They are influenced by their friend's opinions on products and services. They are also influenced by people they don't know but who have credibility as reviewers.

Your ability to influence comes from others, and from you. You can leverage the influence of others to get better clients and bigger sales.

Influence marketing is all about developing a reputation for expertise and credibility in your market while increasing that reputation through strong and meaningful relationships with your target audience.

It's about connecting with your prospects and clients. Influential people communicate effectively with their market because they understand the psychology behind marketing. They know how to influence people's behavior and beliefs about purchasing.

The benefit of developing your ability to use influence marketing isn't only something to do at the personal level. You'll also want to do this in a global manner.

Consider what effect you're trying to produce or what action you want your market to take.

As an influencer, you can expand the reach of your brand. This happens as your opinions and ideas become trusted and acted upon by your target audience.

Wrap your head around this. As we move through this chapter, you'll develop your brand's influence to direct more traffic to your website and sell more experiences of your products and services. You can also direct traffic to build a massive online following to attract deal flow and media attention. Your influence will be a battering ram to open doors for you.

These days, the best way to receive all those benefits is to focus on becoming a social influencer. You can springboard off your reputation in your community while building your credibility and working towards your business goals.

Let me explain what I mean by becoming a social influencer.

Think about a time you've been at a party, and there's that one guy or gal to whom everybody gravitates. Love them or hate them, that person is a social influencer. He or she has developed and refined social skills that are attractive in a party setting. You can apply similar social skills focusing on becoming a social influencer in your industry.

Every decision you make on a daily basis is influenced in some way. This is especially true for our online experiences.

Think about social media websites. We flock to them for that feeling of belonging. Our actions and beliefs are influenced by those perceived as leaders in the group.

Social influence is the power to affect the decisions and actions of others in a social setting. Expert status can be real or may be perceived as real. The test of time will weed out those who aren't providing beneficial advice.

Choose a form of social media relevant to your market. Begin working on building your influence there. I'll explain all the ins and outs of how to do this in the simplest, most effective and powerful way. Because, hey, I'm an expert and I know what I'm talking about!

You'll need strong relationships to influence others. Before this, however, you need to deliver benefits to your followers.

Integrity and honesty form the foundation of your relationships. Your knowledge and how you share your thoughts, opinions, and advice comes second.

It's easier to influence a specialized niche than to dominate a large market. Consider narrowing your first efforts to become an influencer in a small, definable sector.

It's important your brand, which could be your face, your name, or perhaps your corporate identity, be in the forefront at all times.

A confident and dependable image of you and your company is an effective way to create loyalty and trust in your followers. People gravitate toward leaders. They are drawn towards individuals and organizations that show confidence and self-assurance.

Now, like everything else, your market is always changing. To become influential, you also need to learn to be proactive rather than reactive to change. This means you should be someone who takes the lead and initiates change in your market.

Be the brand in your market that's known for doing whatever it takes to be successful. Build your reputation on this. It's an admirable trait for you to share with your followers. It will motivate them to follow your example.

I'm not sure if it's just a showbiz saying, or if you've heard this before, but a quote I remember is that it takes twenty years to become an overnight success. So, before we continue, please know what we're doing isn't an overnight process.

Often like fame, influence achieved quickly is lost just as quickly. You don't want to be someone who has only achieved their fifteen minutes of influence. You need to provide value to your target audience on a regular basis. This way you build and maintain meaningful influence in your market.

As you go down the path of becoming an influencer, don't focus on personal or business goals. When you do what's necessary, providing valuable advice to your market, your ability to influence will come more naturally. Your wants and needs will also be met.

Depending on your market and your current level of expertise, it may take some time for you to impact your industry. This is a good thing. Your consistent track record of solving problems and helping others achieve results will survive a lot longer than any false respect you might earn.

I think I've done a decent job of influencing you to realize you can and should become an influencer. So, how do you create influence? What steps can you take to build your reputation as an expert who helps people in your target market achieve the results they're looking for?

Well, you do that by first understanding the components of influence. When you understand what influence is and how to get, measure, and nurture it, you'll have the formula to be a powerful industry influencer.

The goal of this chapter is to help you improve the strength and the quality of your reputation. Also, to identify opportunities for you to further influence your prospects and clients.

You'll use simple methods to build your reputation as an influential specialist in your market. You'll do this by creating market-appropriate content proves you're an authority in your field.

You'll identify sites online where you need to be, to best grow your sphere of influence.

You'll measure and monitor your influence in your target market and increase your client base and loyalty by reinforcing you as an expert and influential in your field.

As recognition of your credibility increases, your business success will come more easily.

Identify areas where you excel in building influence. Make notes and list your current strengths. List those things that make you a good influencer.

Make sure you take notes so you can quickly refer to them later. This will make putting together your market influence action plan a lot easier when you complete this chapter.

How to Be an Amazing Influencer

It's important for you to recognize, acknowledge, and adopt the mindset top industry influencers share. You also need to understand who and what you're attempting to influence. Determine what niche product, market, service, or topic you'll target in which to become an expert.

As we work on influence, think about specialization rather than generalization.

A brain surgeon earns way more money than a general practitioner; the skills required are more specialized and take longer to master. Beyond that, by specializing in your field, you'll stand out as an expert more so than someone who covers a wide variety of topics.

Nothing is stopping you from becoming an expert in many different areas. You just need to focus and start on one before moving on to another.

By specializing, you'll also build your knowledge and spread your influence faster than if you were to tackle too much at one time. This means you can become a market influencer quickly when you target a smaller marketplace or area of expertise.

It might be, you only need one specialty. If you want to cover broader ground, you can build up your knowledge, skills, experience, and influence in this systemized way to build a solid foundation. Then, expand in an organic way as you grow your expertise. That's what I've being doing over the years.

This is something you need to do proactively. It requires your consistent, ongoing, and active participation to be effective.

You should always think about how you can be of service and be known as a useful source of valuable information.

Have tenacity when it comes to answering questions, solving problems, and giving recommendations. Do this regularly. And remember the golden rule of marketing in the twenty-first century. Before you speak, publish, or create anything, make sure it focuses on the interest of your target market and not your personal interests and desires.

Here are some of the most effective, proven strategies successful industry influencers have used to get where they are today.

In many cases, I'm all for the fake-it-to-make-it philosophy, by diving into something and committing yourself to following through. This isn't viable though, as an industry influencer. People will either see through you right away or the moment you run out of steam.

When networking and socializing, pay attention and focus your mind on discovering what you need to know to become an expert in your field. Do an honest evaluation of where you are now regarding your capacity to take on that leader role in your market.

You might find, one or more of the social networks don't provide enough value for your time invested. Similarly, they may not be as enjoyable for you to take part in. Figure that out quickly and then invest your time where you can learn the most.

Keep in mind, online forums and groups are full of passionate and dedicated people who discuss every detail of a particular niche or topic. So, you have to know your stuff. When you're ready to take on that leadership role, become active in answering questions and solving problems in these forums. This will build your reputation and put you in a position of influence.

Warren Buffett was considered by many to be the smartest stock market investor forty years ago. The same belief was held thirty, twenty, and ten years ago. Today, Mr. Buffett is still seen as the smartest financial mind by many of the world's experts in investing. What is Mr. Buffett's secret to decades as a market influencer?

Warren Buffett has always said ongoing research and education has kept him at the top of the heap in the investing world. Educating yourself on a daily basis is key if you're going to become and remain a major influencer in your field.

Back in my early twenties, for six years, I portrayed Ronald McDonald, the clown. This was on behalf of an advertising agency representing McDonald's restaurants. They hired me because I was a magician, effective at entertaining kids and had (still have) a big goofy smile.

Even when I was a clown, I was still interested in business and marketing. I read a book on the life of Ray Kroc. He said something that has always stuck with me. "When you're green, you grow; when you're ripe, you rot." Words to live by.

Attend local and virtual seminars, conferences, webinars, and listen to podcasts of all different types. Immerse yourself in a variety of sources of specialized information that relate to you and your business.

Brian Tracy is one of the first motivational business speakers I listened to a long time ago, and he is still a favorite thought leader of mine. I remember him referring to an automobile as a rolling university. I also encourage you to take every opportunity you can to learn.

I listen to podcasts when I'm swimming. That's three extra hours a week of learning, thanks to waterproof equipment and the mindset of learning whenever and wherever possible.

Pay most attention to and learn from industry movers and shakers who are considered the authorities in your market. Take their courses, read their books, and attend their seminars.

Regardless of your current level of knowledge and expertise, you can always learn from others. This needs to be something you continue to do if you want to be a true influencer in your market.

Make sure you're up to speed on relevant online and offline trade journals and gather and absorb top-level market information on a daily basis.

Ultimately, you can contribute your content for these journals as you position yourself as a respected authority. Look at this as your first, and a continuing step as you become a well-respected and valuable leader in your market.

You need to be up to date at all times if you want to be a reliable influencer. This means tracking media about your area of expertise. Be selective since there are thousands of newspapers, websites, podcasts, and other forms of media which relate to your market.

I'm not suggesting you spend all your time sifting through this information. Instead, ask others what their top five information sources are in your market. Look for commonalities of sources. Narrow these down. Check them out for yourself and decide which to follow.

There are many websites offering free and paid alert services to track market specific keywords and phrases for you. Anytime these words appear anywhere on the internet, you'll be alerted. You can set up immediate, daily, or weekly alert schedules. This is great, not only to track news information, but to monitor your brand's online reputation.

If you track your name and your brand, then as soon as somebody goes out there and writes about you, either good or bad, you can respond in an effective and immediate way. I use Google Alerts for this.

Remember, stay focused on your specific market and expertise as you go back to the virtual and offline social networks, trade journals, communities, and forums you joined earlier. Then, you'll return to them and share your knowledge.

If you don't have one now, consider starting a blog. By doing this, you gain control of your online presence and total control of your little piece of virtual real estate. You can use this platform to spread your knowledge in whatever way you choose: articles, videos, images, or whatever you want.

You're going out with the mindset of helping and sharing. At the end of the day, you want to draw people into your brand and your service. You want to make sure your brand is noticeable during all your online activities.

Most forums and other online communities allow you to add a signature link to your comments and you should put thought and care into setting this up. Include your logo, your tagline, and your contact information along with a subtle call to action which offers more help.

When sharing your knowledge and expertise, make sure you monitor the effectiveness of your contributions to ensure your content applies to the group and resonates with at least some of them even in a small way at first.

Be visible where it makes sense. Be present where your contributions will help people who gather where you've stepped in to stake your claim as an expert.

If you're looking for ways to position yourself as an industry influencer offline and in your local area, look to Chamber of Commerce organizers who are always looking for speakers to share their knowledge.

This isn't for everyone. If you're already established and looking for ways to boost your credibility and expertise, then it may not be worth your time to speak at Chamber of

Commerce meetings. Although, it would be a nice thing to do as you will be giving back to your community.

I've often recommended to aspiring entertainers and speakers they visit their local Chamber of Commerce. This is an excellent way to network and inexpensively build powerful business relationships. I did it myself when I was starting out as a speaker. It's still an effective business strategy today.

There are plenty of opportunities for you to donate your time, products, and services to local charities. This can also help expand your circle of influence while contributing to your community.

Local meetups are another effective way to connect with people who share your interests. Check out Meetup.com if you're not already involved in that community. You can even start a Meetup group if this appeals to you.

Online, there are guest blogs and websites respected in your market. You can even refer people to other influencers in your area of interest. This becomes reciprocal. In the spirit of giving and sharing, you aren't always going to be the right source for every topic.

Another thing you can easily do is record a podcast. Your goal is to be everywhere and anywhere online and offline that it makes sense for you. Be where your ideal clients gather. As you do this, you become more of a recognized brand.

There was a trend back in the early 2000s when I started in the internet marketing arena. The idea was that a brand should be built around a so-called guru who isn't accessible to the general public. Well, this doesn't cut it today. On the contrary. You want to be out there and available.

When you're getting started with building your reputation, being available is vital. People are turned off by those who become aloof and unavailable. It does make sense for time management and privacy reasons to control how others access you. It's also important you avoid the appearance of hiding from the public.

Being available doesn't mean you give out your cell phone number to anyone you meet. However, there are many ways to be accessible and show you care. You can do this and still protect privacy and manage your time.

One great way to do this is to host free webinars where you're present to interact with your audience. You can interact with your fans and friends. Reply to relevant and constructive tweets. Be on top of your brand communication and be available on a regular basis.

The barriers to being an author have been eliminated by technology. You can self-publish your book and sell it on Amazon. You can sell or give away digital books from platforms like Amazon's Kindle. There are other similar platforms, and new ones all the time. Being an author of a book provides credibility. It can also be a form of passive income and lead generation.

Creating information products like books and courses is a great way for you to deliver solutions to your target audience while quickly becoming a market influencer.

Whether you're creating and publishing blog posts, videos, or digital or printed books, you're now getting the added benefit of building instant authority.

Use direct mail to spread your influence. This used to be one of the only ways other than print ads to direct market. Now, it's really under the radar as the internet has taken over as the primary media for selling products and services directly to consumers and businesses.

Direct mail is relevant here. You can rent lists of people interested in your particular marketplace and mail them gifts, discounts, or other offers. This is a good way to generate business and increase your expert status in a way that few are doing. I can tell you from experience it's not that hard. Return on investment is much higher than online marketing, both in building your expert status and profits for your company.

The acronym SHIP will help you remember the traits of an influencer. SHIP stands for:

Stories – Craft memorable and emotion-provoking stories about yourself and your brand. Share these true-life stories whenever possible.

Help – Always be helpful to those in your market. This means focusing on the needs of prospects, intending to solve their problems and answering their questions.

Integrity – You need to do what you say and operate with the highest set of business and personal ethics. Displaying a high level of ethics is important if you're to become and remain a dependable and reliable influencer.

Passion – Display genuine passion about your market. When others see you're emotionally invested in a certain niche, they'll more likely consider you an expert.

Now, it's time to put what you just learned into action.

Are you ready to define your specialty or target area? This should be an area where you're competent and best suited to assume the role of expert and influencer.

Go to your notes. List the actions you'll take towards implementing each of the strategies from this chapter. Write down how those actions will help you build your credibility, attract more followers, and expand your client base.

How to Spread Your Influence

Communication is the key to being an effective influencer.

To influence the decisions of others, you'll create content that identifies you as an industry authority and expert. But you can't just write a book, publish a few blog posts, or give a presentation at a conference and then stop creating content. Content creation needs to be ongoing. It's a continuous process.

As you deliver content in a consistent and regular manner, it's equally important every piece of content delivers real value. You have to do this to build that perception and reality that you're an important influence in your market.

You're probably noticing a recurring theme, or at least recurring suggestions, of ways to do things as we go through the various chapters of this book.

What do you think the best way is to make sure your message resonates with your prospects in your marketplace? What's the best type of content to establish your expertise and apply your influence over your audience?

I've said it before. Ask your followers. Ask your clients. Asking your audience what they want is the best way to give them what they want.

For example, people eager to learn Pilates or Yoga would likely prefer video over text to teach them how to perform each exercise or pose.

People with very little time to spare may prefer audiobooks and podcasts allowing them to digest your content audibly while they perform other tasks. Like me, when swimming. Other people prefer reading text as a learning medium.

Make sure the content you're delivering is presented in the proper form for your audience. Using more than one format is preferable to reach people with different learning styles.

Creating content that builds your influence also requires consistency. Your email should be formatted the same way each time. If you publish a weekly blog post, make sure it arrives on the same day, at roughly the same time each week. If you build a following via webinars and physical seminars, don't suddenly change to teleconferences and membership groups as a way of getting your content out.

At first, you'll likely experiment and try different things. Once you find what works, realize it works because it's what your audience wants. Don't change it up just because you've discovered a new technology, or you got bored and just want to try something new. It happens all the time. I've done it myself. It rarely works out well to disrupt something that's working well.

As you get started, deliver information to your audience that's factual and reliable. Content representing information that's accepted by the industry will assist in establishing your credibility. Later, you can piggyback on what's already respected, add an opposing point of view, and be known as someone with an opposing opinion. You don't need to always fall in line with what the majority thinks or says.

Develop and follow a purposeful online and offline marketing plan regarding influence building content creation.

You need to be organized about how and when you deliver content to your niche. Stick to a content publication schedule.

Be consistent when it comes to creating and publishing your videos, blog posts, and other content. Follow a plan for visiting forums and groups. Use a pattern to build predictability around the content and information you share to build your brand, your expertise, and your influence.

I mentioned not to rock the boat as you enter these forums and groups with your advice and opinions. However, please understand, I mean this only for when you're starting out.

Ease yourself into a new community and become known before you share daring or more controversial content. Then, by all means, be yourself and express your opposing points of view.

You're special, with unique and distinctive viewpoints based on who you are and what you stand for. People will respect your confidence.

Be yourself and infuse all your content with your personality and attitude. This will allow you to set yourself apart from your competitors. The people who will be drawn to you will be the ones who will help you make more money, help more people, and have more fun.

As a professional performer, you might think it's easy for me to entertain and inspire others while providing useful content. It's more difficult because I need to hold myself back and make sure I'm taken seriously. For that reason, I curb my impulses to crack jokes and make light of things while I'm educating and teaching specific methods and strategies like these.

Entertaining your audience is important. I'm just giving you a word of warning. A little entertainment here and there will keep your audience happy and endear you to them. If you go overboard or use humor which offends or belittles others, you risk alienating people and being perceived as someone who lacks substance.

Creating new content doesn't have to be difficult. You might feel you've run out of ideas. When this happens, look at your old files, documents and emails, blog posts, information products and videos for inspiration.

You can repurpose this information. For example, turn a video into a blog post, or a blog post into a video. Mix up formats and look at old content with a creative mindset. Pay attention to what's new and relevant in the market today.

Your ability to influence others will grow in phases. Not only in general terms but for each client as they move from being a cold or warm lead to doing business with you and continuing to do business with you and referring others to you as well.

For example, when someone first joins your email list, they may not be ready to buy your products or services quite yet.

When creating content, consider connecting with that person according to their place in your buying cycle. This means your opt-in shouldn't be sales oriented and should provide value and actionable information for free. In return, they'll provide an email address for your free content. This is your first phase of influence with that person. You need to court them as you would a first date.

The content you deliver through your email auto-responder continues to offer valuable market-specific information. Your prospect moves deeper into the buying cycle when their trust in you begins to strengthen as you solve their problems and answer their questions.

Think about it, this all relates to the overall theme of this book which is to be client centric. Every phase of your relationship and communication with your prospects and clients is an opportunity for you to provide a relevant and useful experience for them.

Someone who's already entered a business relationship with you by investing in some of your products or services should be provided a very different experience than those who are just checking you out.

Clients who've already purchased from you expect an entirely different type of content. They respect what you have to say and are willing to buy products and services from you. The content you deliver to them must be of an advanced nature, and these people don't mind if that content is sales oriented. In fact, if you've done everything right so far, they not only welcome the invitation to do more business with you but they'll be disappointed if you don't offer them additional opportunities.

Deliver content appropriate not only to your sales cycle but also to your audience's level of market knowledge.

This means, for example, creating free and paid materials and products that make sense for any sales presentation or conference where you're speaking. If you're addressing attendees of a seminar on how to write their first book, the content you deliver for free and extra training or services for purchase needs to apply to authorship or book marketing.

The same is true with virtual relationships. Social networks are less sales oriented than some other internet platforms. Here, you want to give advice, make recommendations, and share product reviews. Make sure you've used the products or services in question and share your real feelings and experiences. Providing your honest opinion when someone is considering making a purchase develops respect and trust.

Every marketplace has a unique language. There are keywords, phrases, and topics specific to each market. We've already covered that in detail in this book. Now, it's time to use industry-specific language and embed those words and phrases into every piece of content you create.

Not only does this make your content consistent and credible, but it also helps search engines find your content. You can also use industry language when you name your products and services.

Earlier, I mentioned being accessible is important. I also shared ways you can do this without compromising privacy.

On social networks, you shouldn't just deliver content for consumption, you should also respond to other's tweets, posts, and comments. Share industry insider's online content and valuable content you find. Just make sure you add your comment or opinion, and when possible, link back to your website or social network page.

Speaking the right language is important online in social networks, and on your website. It's also important offline. In person, you don't have the anonymity of the internet to hide behind. You must speak and deliver content in the language of your marketplace.

There are four characteristics that need to be present for your content to advance the perception you're an industry influencer worth noticing.

These characteristics are:

- Keeping your image consistent.

- Having your content well timed.

- Being present in the right places.

- Presenting your points of view with conviction.

You've already developed a level of expertise and know-how. You may be just starting to carve out a niche as an influential market mover and shaker. You might be a bigwig in your market. Or, you may be somewhere in between.

The key is that your content must coincide with how you're perceived by your market. If you're just establishing yourself as a credible source of information, don't start out by trying to create a definitive guide, answering all problems in your field. You'll be seen as a newbie who doesn't know what they're talking about.

If you're perceived as a veteran authority, make sure the content you deliver reflects that. You always need to provide value. Your content should also match the level of knowledge you have, based on how you're perceived by the marketplace.

What's the most important element of comedy? Timing!

Timing is everything in so many aspects of life. Knowing when to deliver what type of information is crucial to building your image as an influencer. This goes back to understanding your sales cycle. It also applies to non-sales situations as well.

Delivering information when your prospect or client needs it is important for several reasons. For one, it shows you understand your market. Your followers see you know what is and isn't relevant in the marketplace, and when it's important. Well-timed content delivery can help vault you to the top of your market as an industry influencer.

You probably won't sell too many bathing suits in the middle of the desert. But selling umbrellas and ice water in that same situation would be effortless. A fisherman always goes where the fish are. You need to do the same. Constantly and consistently deliver content where your target market lives and breathes.

Have faith in yourself. You know what you're talking about. You've spent a lot of time and effort getting to know your marketplace. When you present your content, do it with confidence.

There are a few things you need to remember concerning content delivery on social networking platforms. At time of this writing, in 2017, if you're selling B2B, you need a quality profile on LinkedIn. If your business is connected in any way to the entertainment industry, your profile and activity on Instagram and Twitter may be important.

Google and the other search engines rank your social media profiles. They study keywords and phrases used in your profiles to help decide how high among their search results you're ranked for those search terms. That's why it's so important to complete all areas of your social media profiles.

Mention your industry accolades, certificates, awards, schooling, and any other achievement which relate to your industry. Don't use just a hundred words for a profile if a particular social network allows a thousand words. This is a simple, free way to expand your industry influence and shouldn't be overlooked.

People search for their interests inside social networks. So, make sure your social media profiles, videos, posts, updates, and tweets are full of industry-specific keywords and phrases.

How is becoming a market influencer like succeeding in real estate investing?

It's all about location, location, location.

I mentioned this earlier, and I can't stress it enough. You need to invest your time where it's best served.

Even though there's scalability and ways to leverage content, building your influence requires your personal time. Time is your most valuable asset. Constantly assess the value of building a presence at specific online and offline venues. Invest most of your time in those that are most beneficial.

Place your focus on the internet to build and grow your influential force in your market. In most cases, a combination of online and offline exposure is the best way to guarantee you're seen as important in your industry.

I know it's not always feasible for people to travel to seminars and conferences, or trade shows in other cities or countries. If this is something you can't or don't want to do, then work on developing an industry presence in your backyard. You can show up at local events, attend, or host meetups or other networking activities. Expand your reach more locally and let it grow organically from there.

Here are different ways you can build your influence locally and grow your business.

There are podcasts which you can host or participate in from your home. Remember to tie in local flavor when targeting your local demographic.

You can also consider developing a local media presence which can provide you, as an authority, thousands of dollars of free advertising or publicity and help build your influence and maybe even celebrity status.

You can attend local conferences. If you live in a major city or near one, there will be plenty of opportunities for you to set up a booth at a trade show. Look for opportunities to attend these events as a volunteer. Many events are looking for presenters, so consider being hired to speak at some of these industry events.

If you're in a smaller city where there are no gatherings specific to your industry, then this is a great opportunity for you to step in and fill that void. Host a conference or seminar. This can change how you're perceived in your field in your local market. I did exactly that when I hosted an internet marketing seminar in Vancouver in 2003.

Let's revisit podcasts. They are suited for the internet as a way of building an audience. They can also deliver offline rewards. If you record a podcast in your local area, you can use this as a way to interview and educate people in your target market. This shows you as both a local celebrity and a knowledgeable local market leader. You can start a podcast with nothing more than your laptop (or phone) and a decent microphone. This portability allows you to move the location of your podcast for each episode, continually growing your market presence.

Local charities are always looking for help raising money. There are also religious organizations, schools, and for-profit companies in your area that would appreciate your help to meet their business goals. Just remember, be selective when choosing a partner in any joint venture campaign.

The right partnership can benefit both parties and develop long-term relationships that solidify your position as an influential force in your market. Selecting the wrong partner can be a waste of your time and efforts, delivering a crushing blow to your reputation in a worst-case scenario.

I learned this the hard way and made several mistakes in this area over the years. Be very cautious when aligning yourself with other individuals and organizations.

I'm now very cautious about joint ventures, even when it comes to simply allowing other people to represent my products or services in the marketplace. Having said that, there's plenty of growth potential in that area. There are many great people with whom you could partner. Just tread cautiously.

Consider your local media. Getting on local radio and television programs is easier than you might think. This is a powerful way for you to build your influence. Shows are constantly looking for people to interview and for on-air contributors.

You can also look at your local newspaper and alternative magazines as a place for you to contribute your content, your knowledge, your expertise, and build your audience and credibility.

Whether you're an optometrist, dog trainer, insurance salesperson, real estate agent, mortgage broker, entertainer, or speaker, appearing in various media will pay you back over and over again. Regardless of your industry or market, your local newspaper, radio, and television stations are there and available for you to share your knowledge with their audience and grow your market influence.

Are you excited about the idea of becoming a media star?

I hope so.

How to Measure Your Influence

Think about what you hope to gain from your efforts. Consider the best-case scenario for you in the next six months, year, and five years down the road.

What do you want to accomplish as an industry influencer? Brainstorm answers to this question. Give yourself a good amount of time to think this through. Doing so will help lay the foundation for your efforts and allow you to look back to see results. It will also enable you to know where to make any necessary adjustments, to help you get where you want to be.

I'm always looking at various ways to measure marketing returns. Use metrics to measure your business. The most common mistake I see is when people waste time on activity that results in little or no impact.

Without having goals in place and knowing what to measure you might build brand recognition, even earn respect and admiration, yet not realize financial returns.

Set specific goals and put measurable performance trackers in place. This way you'll know if your sales and profits are improving along with your industry influence.

You can judge a level of market influence by tracking the percentage of sales that comes from word-of-mouth referrals and return clients. If a significant portion of your sales is generated this way, that's a good indicator you're doing things right. This is something you need to track regularly, month by month, year by year. In this way, you'll know if your level of influence is increasing or decreasing based on these numbers.

Being influential, in most cases, means being an expert in your field. Ask for feedback from your clients and other market influencers. Determine if you're viewed as having significant knowledge and industry expertise. Consistently review who's reaching out to you for help.

Record the occasions where you're invited to important marketing functions, conferences, and seminars. If someone enters your sales funnel and doesn't end up buying from you, ask them why. All of these exercises help you determine if you're viewed as an influential market expert.

Online exit polls are given to clients right after they have made a purchase. You can also survey prospects and others in your market who haven't bought anything from you.

Surveys are a powerful form of market research. Everyone likes expressing their opinion. This is a very direct and inexpensive way to see if you're viewed as credible, trustworthy, and knowledgeable in your field.

Surveying other market influencers can reveal meaningful industry best practices.

Thanks to the internet, it's possible to arrive at a number which shows your social score. Online, you can easily find different applications and websites which grade how you're perceived on the most important social networking sites.

Internet search engines rank web pages in order of authority and relativity regarding a specific search term. Higher rankings are viewed as more believable and authoritative.

Becoming an industry influencer can lead to consistent and sustainable business success. Whether you have a brick and mortar or virtual business, the proven methods covered in this chapter will help you become an expert at influence marketing.

When you establish market influence, you're viewed with respect and admiration in your field, leading to personal and business goals and advantages being realized.

CHAPTER SIX: PERSUASION MARKETING

Persuasion is a skill that's different from influence and different from selling.

If you're struggling with the idea of selling, this chapter will rid you of all your worries in that area.

You know I'm a big believer in building a strong foundation based on goals which tie into your strategies. Sales and marketing tactics are built upon that foundation to leverage and boost your effectiveness.

In the past, I've taken the approach of providing a harder type of sell, using hyperbole in sales letters and overusing scarcity tactics and other methods to persuade people to take action.

I did those things with good intentions. I believed I should do anything to persuade someone to do business with me because I knew it was in their best interest. And why wouldn't I give it my best shot since I know it's what they need and I have a strong desire to grow my business?

Times have changed. Those strategies are no longer that effective, and I'm no longer comfortable with them. I've learned we'll be far more successful in the long run if we make sales based on a different approach. That approach is to sell the experience, as opposed to selling products and services. This client centric approach is hypnotic in nature.

I don't think anybody enjoys being hard sold or even gently pressured. I now view this as a negative experience. Hard selling is the opposite of what I'm teaching in this book.

If you fear being seen as a used car salesperson or carnival huckster, but feel those tactics are viable, throw those thoughts away. You don't need them. You'll be far more successful learning and applying the persuasive selling methods in this chapter. These methods are far more comfortable, more effective, and are in the best interests of your clients.

The reality is your clients are the foundation of your business. Selling your products and services to them is the reason your company exists.

You need not feel uncomfortable about persuading people to do business with you. Use methods to convince others in a way that's natural. By doing so, the selling process will no longer be scary or painful.

If you don't find the sales process daunting, you'll still find these new methods shared in this chapter are powerful additions to your arsenal. They should be adopted by you to attract, keep, and grow more clients so you can make more money, have more fun, and help more people.

That's what it's all about. You can't make more money, have more fun, and help more people if you don't have a business. The more you can persuade people to do business with you, the more people you can help, the more money you can make, and the more fun you can have.

Marketing Magic

To be successful in show-business, I needed to be both a professional entertainer and marketing expert. I discovered early on, these two parts of show and business were equally important.

For decades, my marketing efforts focused on persuading people to book my shows. My success was due to a solid performance both on and off stage. This approach, combined with persuasive marketing methods and being client centric, made for an amazing career.

It was 2001 when I dove into the world of internet marketing. I traded my rabbit for a mouse. Focusing more on training than performing magic, I taught online marketing at seminars and through my books and courses.

You can't use all the same marketing tactics that worked back in 2001. Sometimes you cannot use tactics that were viable last month. Things change fast today. Attitudes and behavioral patterns of your clients have changed. Old marketing methods and techniques have to evolve, or you'll no longer be relevant as a brand.

During the last few decades, we've endured a flood of sales and marketing material. I remember going to movies where I didn't have to watch commercials before the film. There are screens in taxicabs, and digital and print advertising and marketing material everywhere you turn. It's even more rampant online. Because of being inundated with these ads, we learn to tune out and ignore exaggerated language and the hype.

I remember when banners were a new thing online. In response, we as a society developed what is called banner blindness. Banners were no longer effective after a few years. However, things keep changing. Now there are ways to use banners again. Be aware there are cycles with what works in marketing, just as there are cycles with music, fashion, and many other things.

The online versions of used car salesmen apply tactics which to most people are transparent and obvious. The people applying these tactics are opportunists looking to make a quick buck. They have little regard for the client's best interest.

Most consumers aren't responsive to this approach anymore. They are smarter, and they understand and recognize when they're being manipulated.

Old-school sales techniques of the past only viewed clients as a way to make a quick sale. As marketers today, we need to build relationships and provide experiences. Our goal is for our client to see us as a trusted friend and source for valuable information. People want to feel like they're a part of the brands they love and not just a number in the company's marketing plan.

The real key to building relationships is simple. It's to focus on your client's needs. When you listen to them, you can understand their problems and desires. You can then offer products and services they seek.

That's what the essence of persuasion marketing is. It's an integral part of teaching you how to provide an amazing client experience.

I assume you aren't interested in the sale of products or services to people who lack an interest in what you're promoting. With that in mind, let's focus on how to attract and retain clients for whom you'll add value. This way you won't need to rely on convoluted sales tactics to persuade them to do business with you.

As with everything else, there's a particular way to do this. We'll dig into that in a meaningful way in this chapter.

One approach savvy marketers use to reach their audience online is through content marketing. Your clients are looking online for information, and you need to be there to provide it.

In the last chapter, we talked about how you can build your expertise and become a trusted provider by answering questions and influencing people once you've established yourself as an authority in your niche. If you do this, you inspire trust as you're building relationships and the resulting sale is an organic result of that relationship.

Your prospecting for new clients occurs as people realize you're offering what they want. They are pre-sold, pre-conditioned to do business with you.

It's not cool any longer to rely on one-way forms of communication, as it was with older marketing channels like television and print media. Now, conversations go both ways. The conversation is more about listening to your clients rather than you talking to them.

Your clients are proactive and going out to find what they want on the internet as opposed to passively watching TV.

Your job as a persuasion marketer is to provide that information. That's your first step in persuading them to do business with you.

In today's environment, your marketing has to be even more client focused than before. It's no longer enough for your website or marketing materials to display how good you are. You also need to emphasize tangible results your clients will get from the products and services you can provide. Back it all up with evidence supporting your claims.

Do your homework and know your target market. You've been prompted to do plenty of this already in this book. I hope by now you have a good sense for your market. When you know what makes your people tick, it's easy to apply persuasion marketing. In fact, it will happen naturally.

Offer them what they want and think they need. Invite them to join the dialogue. During this exchange, they may discover their wants and needs aren't what they thought. This is one way you quickly benefit your clients.

This exploration, for your clients, is valuable for them and can either persuade them to move forward with you or to move on. If it's right for them to move on, you're also doing yourself a favor by qualifying your clients. You're freeing up your resources to deal with those who can benefit from doing business with you.

That's how you build a sustainable long-term business that keeps you happy.

Share Your Expertise

Well, here it is. The first key to successful selling is expertise. Good thing this concept isn't new to you after reading the last chapter.

You already know that an expert is someone who knows more than you do about a particular topic. They have expert status because of their credentials, their visibility, their following, or their quality content.

When you establish yourself as an expert on specific topics, your products and services will virtually sell themselves.

There are many ways to show your expertise, and none of them involve anything dishonest. You need not fake it. We spoke earlier about fake it till you make it. I told you it might have its place in some areas. There's no room for it when planning for a successful and sustainable business.

So, just like when applying influence, in persuasion marketing, you establish yourself as an expert on specific topics.

Now, based on my target marketing for this product, it's a safe bet for me to say you're already established in your niche. This book caters to service providers and professionals looking to expand their business. So, you likely already are an expert and know a lot about your market and have a great level of expertise

If you're looking to expand into other market verticals, the next few pages of information will be especially valuable to you.

Everything you do in business begins with your niche. You start with something you already know about based on your education, training, personal experience, or your interests.

If you've had serious, positive relationships in your life, you may have chosen to become a relationship expert. If you're an avid reader of self-help books, you may turn that interest into an area of expertise. Or, your job in the security industry allows you to have insight into security issues most people don't know about.

Look at your areas of knowledge and experience and seek out the golden nuggets of information you can share. You may find you have more knowledge and expertise than you realize. With this in mind, you'll find new ways to share your knowledge even if it's only in your existing field of specialization.

If you don't want to focus on an area you already know about, another method of niche selection is to choose a topic you'd like to learn about. It doesn't matter if you're not an expert already. If you put in the time to learn about it, you can become an authority on that topic. You can become an expert, and share that knowledge with your audience.

Remember, the expertise gap is the difference between what you know about a particular topic and what your audience knows. This difference is based on what you know, but others haven't yet learned.

Understanding this is an important part of building your current ability to persuade. Understand your clients and their level of knowledge about your topic.

For example, if you've lived abroad for thirty years, you're an expat expert. Write your content for people who are just setting off abroad as you did years ago. Or, if you already know how to set up a basic WordPress site, you can teach others how to do the same.

Your bio should say more than just, "An avid book reader." It must show your expert knowledge and experience. A good way to do this is by building a portfolio. Publish articles wherever you can. Write guest posts for other blogs. Join official organizations and take part in events. Conduct seminars for local groups. Teach classes at local colleges. Write press releases for distribution to online and offline publications.

Create a long list of all the things you've done that show you know your topic well. Then use those to construct a detailed bio or About page on your website.

It's impossible to establish your expertise overnight, especially through authentic means.

It takes time and dedicated effort. Learn about your topic, create lots of content, build your credentials, and grow an audience base. Each year you teach about your subject adds tremendously to your reputation as an expert.

Okay, time to think about what you know others don't, even if it seems basic to you. Assuming you're already working in a particular niche, focus on what you know about that topic.

Then brainstorm ways or places where you can demonstrate your knowledge.

Show Don't Tell

Persuasive selling is never about forcing a product or service down someone's throat and in fact, it's far from it. Especially in today's market, people have more choices than they've ever had before and hard-sell tactics are never a good option. As a salesperson or marketer, you need to demonstrate and educate. Your clients will choose you only if it's right for them.

Demonstrating and educating means giving your clients all the information they need to understand what you're offering, and all the details they need to know about it. This should be the purpose of your sales process and the backbone of persuasion marketing and selling.

Let's look at marketing as teaching. When you do so, you realize you need to educate your prospects about your general topic first. For example, if you're selling health products you need to explain not just the benefits but also how your product will achieve the results your clients want.

With a technical product, you may have to assume your prospects have no prior knowledge. Break complicated subjects into more digestible pieces to help them understand.

To become a master at persuasion marketing, make your brand a go-to for information on everything related to the product or service you offer.

Demonstrating and educating is important. People believe what they see more than what they read. It isn't enough to only tell them what your product does. A good way to do this is to create videos that show your products in use.

Produce videos showing the many uses of your product, especially those not so obvious.

As persuasion marketers, our mission is to be client centric and create amazing experiences for our clients. The last thing we want to do is hide behind any of the weaknesses of our product or service. Other marketers hide or mask the truth about the weakness of their products. This isn't a wise approach.

We want our clients to make the right decision, especially in the service business. If someone buys a product or engages your service, and it doesn't suit their needs, there's a good chance they'll ask for a refund. They may not do business with you again. This has a real cost to your business in reputation, time, energy, and money.

Present the advantages and the disadvantages of your brand, your services and products. This provides your prospects with a fair representation and helps them make the right decision. It also fosters trust, a key component in persuasion.

If you're honest with people and provide full disclosure of what you offer, your prospects are more likely to do business with you. They are more likely to stay with you for the long run.

We don't want to engage people for who we aren't the right solution. Keep in mind those prospects aren't right for us either. Remember the eighty-twenty rule.

Now, this doesn't mean you have to present any disadvantages in a negative light. When talking about the pros and cons of your product or service, you can discuss how the pros outweigh the cons. Or you can explain the relative unimportance of any downsides based on your target audience's needs. The key is to address any potential objections in advance so people can decide whether moving forward with you will solve their problem or fill their need.

Make sure your website has a Frequently Asked Questions (FAQ) page or information resource page. Anticipate what you may be asked and prepare answers in advance. Post the questions and answers as a resource for your clients. When you get customer service calls or emails, use that as an opportunity to add to your questions and answers list.

Videos are effective for educating potential clients. Other effective methods include eBooks, reports, webinars, newsletters, and blogs. Use different media formats. Remember, some people are more receptive to certain types of media than others.

You can never provide too much information. And the right amount of information is whatever it takes to answer all of your prospects questions. You need to create a wide variety of content to show your audience what you can do.

Additional content further demonstrates how your product or service can solve their problems. Clients have a variety of questions when they're shopping, and your goal is to create a one-stop resource for them. Provide the answers they need to make informed and intelligent purchasing decisions.

Make a list of potential and current questions your clients have about your product or service. Think about and list any of the past or possible objections they may have about going forward with you.

It wouldn't hurt for you to have a look at your competitor's resource pages or FAQ pages. Brainstorm various ways to answer each question.

Make a list of questions you'll answer. Now, draft out an answer for each. Make it easy for your clients to get more answers when needed.

Writing great sales copy is a valuable skill. I'll paraphrase a quote by John Lennon. He said if he wants to build a new swimming pool, he just has to write a new song to pay for it. The ability to write persuasive sales copy can also act as a license to print money.

People with an ability to write persuasive sales copy can sell pretty much anything to select groups of people. This can be a dangerous skill in the wrong hands. The most effective way to persuade people through sales copy is to be straightforward, truthful, and informative.

We went into great detail on storytelling earlier in this book. Hopefully, you've been preparing your stories to share. That groundwork will pay off for you here again. Great sales copy becomes more persuasive when you tell a story that resonates with your audience.

Honest sales copy tells the reader what they need to know about the product or service. The best sales copy answers questions before they are asked.

When you write your sales copy, put yourself in the shoes of your reader and ask, "What do I need to know before engaging these services or buying this product?"

Persuasive copy doesn't just describe features. It also outlines the tangible benefits these features offer the client. Don't expect your client to fill in the blanks. They'll read your copy with skepticism. You have to explain to them how what you offer will achieve the benefits they desire.

For example, let's imagine you're selling a mattress made with NASA technology that molds to your body's shape. The result is you get a better night's sleep. It fits your shape, so you're less likely to wake up in the middle of the night to change position.

For each feature, tell the client why and how it helps them. What's obvious to you may not be to others not as familiar with your product or service.

Since you're trying to drive home the benefits and results for your client, show them evidence to back up your claims. Show them how you've helped others. This will give them an idea of how you'll help them. This is called social proof, and it lends credibility to your statements.

What you need are honest testimonials from clients and to get them, all you need to do is ask. If a client is happy with you, they'll be delighted to share with others.

You can offer incentives like a free sample, a discount, or another special deal, but stress to the client you want their honest thoughts and feelings.

Make sure they understand they aren't obligated to give you a good review.

Sales copy written in a conversational style will be more persuasive. Avoid language that's stiff, formal, or exaggerated. Exaggerated sales copy sounds suspicious or dodgy to most people. Your text should be written as though coming from a good friend or family member. One way to keep your writing style in line is to record yourself reading it and listen to the recording.

That's how I do most of my writing. Then, you'll need to go back and carefully edit, as I'm doing right now. Several times!

Make your written copy easy to scan. The reader should skim through the text and get the gist of it. Break up text into bullet points, small paragraphs, and short sentences. Give each section a headline summarizing the message of the section.

Honest sales copy is persuasive sales copy. It also allows the reader to trust you. When clients know you're honest with them, they are much more likely to be persuaded in your direction.

Make a list of the benefits and features of your product or service. Then make a list of potential sources of proof of the benefits. These sources of evidence can be from your clients or other reputable sources.

Explain your product or service to at least two friends who fit your client market. Listen to the questions they ask. Make a note of how you can better explain your product or service.

Then do this same exercise again. Each time improve your message.

Persuasive Story Telling

We all know the best marketing tells a story.

People love stories. Like a movie or book, a good marketing story has a plot, characters, and movement toward a climax. It keeps people reading and hanging on to see what will happen next.

Because we've gone over this in great detail already in this book, I'm now going to offer new content and viewpoints on storytelling as they relate to persuasion.

If you look at almost any story, you'll see a typical structure. This structure consists of setting, situation, and solution. These are the three S's of story structure.

The setting gives a background for the story. The situation is the challenge the characters must overcome. The solution is usually the happy ending where a problem is solved.

Personal stories work well to sell products and services. A personal story may relate how you struggled with a problem similar to that faced by your listener. You figured out a solution, which was solved by the product or service you offer.

Goods and services that were made to address a problem typically have personal stories behind them.

Even if it's not your story, somewhere, there's a personal story involved.

It's likely you connected with that personal story, which is why you're where you are today as a provider of your product or service.

A variation on the personal story involves an expert who helped you solve the problem. The story is the same, but in this case, you leverage the expert's story and knowledge.

This type of story is compelling because of the air of mystery surrounding the expert. The expert may be inaccessible to your audience. However, you are accessible.

You can introduce your prospects to the expert and let them tell their story themselves. This approach is perfect for webinars and teleseminars.

You can add some history or culture to your product or service to reframe it. Remember at the beginning of this book when we talked about reframing as related to mindset? Reframing is powerfully persuasive and is common with natural health products using indigenous traditional medicine.

The setting for a story featuring an herb's use for thousands of years among the people of the Amazon Basin helps to explain to the client where it's coming from and why they should try it.

The product doesn't just appear out of the blue.

In addition to the story of your products and services, it also helps to have a story about yourself as it relates to your product or service.

Celebrity marketers with large followings usually have a good back story. Other common internet marketing stories include:

The single mother who built an online business while raising her kids.

The slacker or surfer who achieved nothing much in life but discovered an easy way to make money online.

The stressed executive who left the rat race to change the world.

Just remember, your story needs to be real to be effective. Never make up a story as an attempt to persuade people.

There's never any need to fabricate your story. Every person, and every product, has a story behind it whether you realize it or not. Instead of creating a history out of thin air, look for the one that's already there waiting to be discovered. Start by looking at the obstacles you had to overcome and how you did it.

Peer Persuasion

Social proof isn't a secret underground persuasion technique. It's a simple concept that anyone can use to boost their sales. It works because clients are much more likely to buy something others have bought.

There's nothing more influential in buying decisions than word of mouth.

Social proof takes many forms. One example is the client testimonial. Effective sales pages have testimonials interspersed with product information. Social proof could be endorsements from experts, celebrities, and other influencers. In the world of social media, it can be likes, retweets, shares, and further publication of your content and blog comments.

When you make a purchase, there's often uncertainty and risk. The product could fall short of its promises. It may not be what you expected. Shopping online is riskier than shopping offline because you can't see the product up close. Social proof reduces this risk. If others bought the product, and it lived up to its promise, you may be persuaded to believe you'll enjoy similar results.

Even social proof has to emphasize benefits. A review of a dog training book, for example, needs to do more than just say it's a book full of useful information. An effective client testimonial might say useful information from the book resulted in the client having their dog sitting, rolling over, and begging that very afternoon. If someone else got those results, then you can too!

A review of a cosmetic surgeon or skin treatment facility would do more than saying they feel and look younger. It would describe how the specific guidance and procedures led to greater confidence. How this translated into higher sales in business. And, how it helped them socially meet more attractive people. Now, that's a persuasive testimonial.

An even better form of social proof is to show visible results. Clients are often willing to create a video talking about or demonstrating the benefits of your product or service. Also, consider before and after images. These are frequently used to show the advantages of a product or service.

If you want client testimonials, it's just a matter of asking for them. Clients who enjoyed your product will be happy to share the good news with others. You might send them a message after their purchase asking them to write a testimonial if they liked the product. Another good time to ask is when a client emails you with positive feedback. Here, you can ask to use the actual email, which means they don't have to do anything at all.

Another way to get testimonials is to offer freebies, discounts, or a limited-time offer. Some clients need a little nudge, and this is a good way to encourage them. You can give away samples of the product and ask for feedback as a testimonial. Giving out free sample copies of your book or product is also a good way to get an endorsement. I've done this many times.

Social media activity is persuasive social proof. People use social media sites to learn about products they want to buy. This is why companies put resources into building their social media presence, creating profiles, and getting clients engaged.

Use any negative feedback you get as a way to identify where you can possibly make improvements in your products or their delivery.

When you get positive feedback, you can use that to tell other potential buyers what your products will do for them.

Persuasion by Removing Risk

Giving away freebies is a powerful marketing strategy, but it runs counter to the logic of selling. Why give things away for free when you could make money with them? Giving away freebies is an investment and a long-term strategy that translates to more sales down the road. The benefits are worth the effort, and it can be done without much cost.

When you give something to someone for free, they feel obligated to give something back. They may not immediately buy from you, but they'll be much more open to your marketing persuasion.

This is a simple concept in human relationships called reciprocity. If I buy you dinner for no other reason than the fact I'm in a good mood, you'll feel like returning the favor next time. You would, wouldn't you?

There are additional benefits to giving away freebies than just sales. When you give out freebies, it helps you get exposure. A free eBook you offer can have a link to your site on the footer of each page. You can encourage your readers to share it with their friends and then you'll get even more exposure.

Your giveaways help you establish your expertise and therefore be more persuasive. Your audience gets a taste of the high-quality content you offer. They see you as a knowledgeable person who's here to help, rather than a marketer or salesperson trying to make a sale. Giving away something for free also exceeds their expectations. Exceeding expectations is always amazing.

Almost anything can be a good gift to give away. Physical products aren't typically used as pure giveaways because of the costs of production and shipping. However, small and inexpensive promotional items can work well.

It's common for online marketers to give away a free information product. This could be an eBook, a report, a resource guide, a video series, a cheat sheet, etc.

Whatever format it takes, the idea is to give the clients a taste of your high-quality content while solving one of their problems at the same time. Best of all, information products cost little to produce, there are no shipping costs, and much of the distribution process can be automated.

Another good persuasive idea that costs nothing is offering a free trial. This is how software companies often make sales. After thirty days of using the product for free, the client realizes it is helpful and buys it.

They know firsthand that it meets their needs. You can also offer a free trial for a membership site or other subscription service.

If you have a continual stream of freebies, giveaways, and discounts that are offered through your site and email list, you keep your clients tuned in to see what's coming next. It builds your reputation as a friendly source of quality information.

When they purchase the goods or services you're offering, you'll be at the top of their mind and will be the one they go to first. That's how you become a persuasive marketer.

Persuasion Using Scarcity

Scarcity is a technique used by marketers to persuade people to take action. It's not a comprehensive method by itself. All the other elements of good marketing need to be in place first. It won't sell your product or service for you, but it will increase your sales by urging your clients to act now.

There are two main types of scarcity used by persuasion marketers: limited quantity and limited time.

Limited quantity means there are only a certain number of units for sale, and only a few left. For example, you may offer just five more spots in your new membership site. Once those five are filled, you won't take on any new members for a while. If clients want to join your site, they'll have to act fast.

An example of time limits would be to offer a discount on your services, but only for the next forty-eight hours. Once that deadline comes, the deal is off. Again, the client knows they need to act fast to get the benefits of your offer.

There are basic guidelines for using scarcity fairly. Follow through on your limit. If the deal is only good for this week, stick to only this week. Don't make exceptions, or else the tactic won't work as well next time. People will know it's a false threat. You'll lose steam in your efforts to persuade.

Try using scarcity at the end of your sales funnel. Pre-qualify your clients and get them interested before you tell them there are only five left in stock, or limited dates available.

When using scarcity, always give a good reason for it. This shows your clients you're not being disingenuous or manipulating them. Justifying scarcity is tough when you sell online products such as eBooks, which don't exist physically. However, what I often do is offer my books at a low price as an introduction for readers. Another option is to sell your current book before it's removed from the market when your new book comes out.

Limited quantities and limited time aren't the only ways to use scarcity. You can give a freebie to the first X number of clients who buy your product. This is often called the early bird special, and it rewards them for taking action quickly.

Special products could only be made available for list members and social media fans. They get offers that non-members don't get. This technique uses scarcity to create an exclusive club, and it raises the perceived value of your offerings.

You can also offer a free trial, during which people get a discount for buying. Once the free trial is over, the product goes back up to its regular price.

Using scarcity in persuasion marketing leads to some justified objections. One is that we're using fear or stress to force people into buying what they don't need. Scarcity gets people off the fence. Procrastination is one of the biggest sales killers.

You're offering something that will solve your client's problem. Scarcity is just a little nudge to get them buying. It's also an excellent opportunity to provide extra incentives that make buying your product or committing to your service more valuable to them.

Persuasion Through Repetition

There's a good reason salespeople hammer their clients with their marketing message over and over again. It's persuasive.

Most people don't buy products or services the first time they hear about them, so this repetition is necessary. The more you repeat things, the better they sink in. The more you repeat things, the better they sink in. See what I did there?

There are many reasons it's good to repeat your marketing message, even if you feel you're beating it to death. In today's busy world, there's a lot of static noise. People often miss things. Repeating your message helps it stick.

Your clients may not understand your message the first time they hear it. They may not be ready to hear it. Situations change, and they may need your product or service at a later date. If you sell internet security software, for example, a person's interest level will transform once their site is hacked.

Repetition is also an essential element of branding. It links you with your message. It helps create consistency.

To be effective with repetitive messages isn't as easy as you might imagine. It requires creativity, or else it's just more irritating noise. To keep your message interesting, deliver it as many ways as possible. Create text-based marketing materials, videos, or visual content like infographics. Use as many media formats as possible.

Mix up your use of marketing channels. For example, use your blog, social media, television, and radio. This allows you to persuade people who are hanging out in different venues. You may feel you're repeating your message over and over, but different people hear it each time.

Try to approach the problem that your product or service solves from several angles. Create your materials targeting different clients who need your services.

If you offer SEO services, for example, you may try targeting busy website owners who don't have time to do their SEO, even though they could. Also, there are website owners who have no clue about how to do SEO. You can persuade both these potential clients through repetitive, yet different ads.

Clients have different questions when they research products. One type of answer may not address their issues while another one will.

There's such a thing as too much repetition, especially if you're not varying your message enough. On the internet, people choose what marketing they want to see. It's not like the old days of television before we had PVR's where they had no choice but to sit through commercials. If you say too much of the same thing, they'll tune you out. Even worse, you may be accused of spamming.

Make a list of potential places, or channels, where you can communicate your marketing message with different forms of content. Make sure these channels are accessed by your prospects and clients.

For each channel, note which segments of your market congregate there, and which ones have the highest number of prospective clients reading, listening, or watching. These channels will provide the greatest return on investment.

Select three to five channels for focusing your marketing message or other content marketing. Make a note of which types of clients you're targeting in each channel.

Are you ready to get out there with your new persuasive marketing skills? By this point, you have enough information to be more persuasive right away.

It's time to get serious about persuasive marketing and do it in a way that will help you grow your business.

CLAIM YOUR FREE GIFT

Thank you for reading *Client Centric*. I hope it was both enjoyable and inspirational. More importantly, it's my sincere desire to make changes in the way people relate to their clients. Hopefully, you'll be part of this positive movement.

Regardless of our business or profession, we're all salespeople. Our job is to sell the experience of doing business with our brand.

The lessons in this book are primarily foundational versus tactical. With your foundation in place, it's faster, easier, cheaper, and more efficient when applying marketing tactics.

Your next step is to act on what you've learned in this book. Then, stay up to date on marketing methods to further build upon your foundation. As you do, your business will become client centric. You'll grow your business by delivering an amazing client experience.

To help you further, I have a special gift just for you, my dear client and reader of *Client Centric*. It's waiting for you right now at:

RandyGift.com/ccbook

ABOUT THE AUTHOR

Randy Charach is an entrepreneur, author, speaker, and entertainer. He has founded a variety of successful companies in diverse industries, becoming a self-made millionaire by the age of twenty-four.

Randy is an in-demand keynote speaker and corporate business trainer. He shares his proven effective methods related to sales, marketing, branding, focus, and the customer experience.

Uniquely talented, Randy is a professional comedian, mentalist, magician, and hypnotist. He has performed thousands of live shows across six continents.

Randy has written several best-selling books, courses, and online-learning programs. He has contributed to dozens of print and online publications.

Randy is a guest on CNN and many other notable media outlets. Overall, he has appeared as an entertainer, expert, and media personality on over one hundred radio and television programs.

To discover more of what Randy offers, visit

RandyCharach.com